ROUTLEDGE LIBRARY EDITIONS: THE GOLD STANDARD

Vol

T0271855

TEN YEARS OF CURRENCY REVOLUTION

ROUTLEDGE LIBRARY EDITIONS
THE GOLD STANDARD

Volume 7

TEN YEARS OF
CURRENCY REVOLUTION

TEN YEARS OF CURRENCY REVOLUTION

1922–1932

CHARLES MORGAN-WEBB

Routledge
Taylor & Francis Group

LONDON AND NEW YORK

First published in 1935 by George Allen & Unwin Ltd

This edition first published in 2018
by Routledge
2 Park Square, Milton Park, Abingdon, Oxon OX14 4RN

and by Routledge
711 Third Avenue, New York, NY 10017

Routledge is an imprint of the Taylor & Francis Group, an informa business

British Library Cataloguing in Publication Data
A catalogue record for this book is available from the British Library

ISBN: 978-1-138-56184-7 (Set)
ISBN: 978-1-351-24702-3 (Set) (ebk)
ISBN: 978-1-138-57911-8 (Volume 7) (hbk)
ISBN: 978-0-8153-6525-9 (Volume 7) (pbk)
ISBN: 978-1-351-26212-5 (Volume 7) (ebk)

Publisher's Note
The publisher has gone to great lengths to ensure the quality of this reprint but
points out that some imperfections in the original copies may be apparent.

Disclaimer
The publisher has made every effort to trace copyright holders and would welcome
correspondence from those they have been unable to trace.

TEN YEARS OF CURRENCY REVOLUTION

1922–1932

by

SIR CHARLES MORGAN-WEBB
M.A., C.I.E.

LONDON
GEORGE ALLEN & UNWIN LTD
MUSEUM STREET

Published in the U.S.A. under the title "The Money Revolution"

FIRST PUBLISHED IN 1935

CONTENTS

CONTENTS

FOREWORD

A PRELIMINARY estimate of the momentous nature of
the Currency Revolution outlined in this volume can
be obtained by comparing the passage from the Report
of the Cunliffe Commission quoted on page 59 with
the passage from the British Empire Currency
Declaration quoted on page 200. They are both
authoritative expositions of British currency policy.
But they appear to have emanated from different
worlds, in different ages. They are separated by an
interval of fifteen years only, 1918 to 1933; and yet
the word "revolutionary" is the only possible term
to use to describe the profound differences between
the currency policies they proclaim. The Cunliffe
Report exhibits a callous and supercilious indifference
to internal prosperity and welfare, only conceivable
in the light of Mr. Montagu Norman's subsequent
confession that the Bank of England had previously
had no direct contact with the position of industry
in the country. From this position of serene aloofness
the Cunliffe Report regarded trade, industry, commerce, employment, wages, prices, profits, and prosperity as mere cogs in the automatic machine which
regulated the operation of the Gold Standard.

But the British Empire Currency Declaration of
1933, instead of regarding trade, industry, and commerce as subsidiary factors to be used for the supreme
objective of maintaining the gold reserves of the Bank

of England, boldly reversed the Cunliffe policy, and in a magnificent and memorable sentence declared that for the future the aim of the currency policy of Britain would be to maintain an equilibrium price level that would secure three objectives:

1. To restore the normal activity of industry and employment;
2. To ensure an economic return to the producer of primary commodities;
3. To harmonise the burden of debts and fixed charges with economic capacity.

Currency, in brief, is to be the handmaid of trade, commerce, and industry, not their capricious and despotic tyrant.

If any justification is needed for the publication of this book, it is provided by the debate on currency in Parliament on December 21, 1934. It was possible for Mr. Amery (a former Secretary of State) to make a lamentable confession of ignorance of the contents and nature of the two important official announcements which are reproduced as Appendices I and II to this volume. He stated that Parliament had not received "a clear statement of the economic policy of the Government, and particularly their policy with regard to the monetary situation." Mr. Neville Chamberlain replied with telling effect that the financial policy of Britain, and indeed of the British Empire, had been declared at the close of the London Conference (Appendix II), that it had not been materially changed since then, that it had been successful, and that, if continued, "it would do more to overcome the inharmonious elements which are to be found in the currency systems of the world to-day than anything else."

The reference of Mr. Neville Chamberlain to this Declaration recalls the fact that after I had published a previous book,[1] several friends expressed extreme surprise at the revolutionary nature of the passages I had quoted from it. I was also informed that there was a surprising ignorance in the City as to the policy outlined in the Declaration, and not a little scepticism that such a document existed. The depth of obscurity into which it had fallen may be demonstrated in a simple manner. It contains two grave errors—misrepresentations of what the Ottawa Conference had recommended. Had the Declaration been taken seriously in the City these errors would have been immediately detected and exposed. But so completely has it been disregarded that they have remained undetected for eighteen months after its publication. A reference to pages 198 and 210 of this volume will indicate the serious nature of the errors made when the Declaration was issued.

A comparison between Appendices I and II affords a striking demonstration of the manner in which the provisional Commodity Standard, tentatively introduced at Ottawa, found congenial soil, took deep root, and in the eleven intervening months flourished far

[1] *The Decline and Fall of the Gold Standard.*

beyond the anticipations of those responsible for its introduction.

An even more interesting comparison can be instituted between Appendices I, II, and III. Appendix III reproduces President Roosevelt's famous message to the World Economic Conference on July 3, 1933. It is worthy of reproduction, not so much because it is currently believed to have been the instrument which brought the World Economic Conference to an untimely end, but because it enunciates a currency policy identical with that adopted for the British Empire eleven months previously. It is a remarkable testimony to the psychology of the Press that President Roosevelt's message achieved fame because it was regarded as being destructive. But the Monetary Resolution of the Ottawa Conference, which was constructive, which proclaimed identically the same currency policy as that of President Roosevelt's message, which effected the most momentous Currency Revolution the world has experienced since Britain adopted the Gold Standard in 1816, was allowed to fall into oblivion. It was relegated when issued, in small print, to a subsidiary page of *The Times* with the disparaging remark—"it does not suggest any spectacular methods for dealing with the position." The best method of instituting the comparison between Appendices I, II, and III is to compare each of them with *The Times* summary of President Roosevelt's message quoted on page 194 of this volume. It forms an excellent summary of the currency policy embodied in each of the three documents.

Appendix IV is included, not only because it gives the first authoritative description of the operation of the Exchange Equalisation Fund published in Britain, but also because it contains a spirited defence of British currency policy made by an eminent American banker in a somewhat critical environment. Such a generous tribute to British capacity for currency administration is all the more welcome after the deplorable lapse from currency sanity on the part of Britain between the years 1925 and 1931.

In my previous book the publishers of one of the American Editions inserted a blue slip at page 130 with an inscription at the top reading "Chapter X—Begin reading here." This is, I understand, the first instance on record in the publishing world in which the publishers, on recommending a book to the public, have invited its readers to skip the first nine chapters. The remaining three chapters must have been of peculiar potency, for they put one American Professor of Economics in such a panic that he wrote to Sir Josiah Stamp informing him of "the tendency of such material to mislead the President and people of this country." I admit the soft impeachment that President Roosevelt did read the book (most probably only the last three chapters), and would add furthermore that he expressed his appreciation of its exposition of British Currency Policy.

In reply to the timorous professor, Sir Josiah Stamp stated:

the adoption of a commodity standard is not the policy of the Government;

and:

no official steps have been taken by the Government towards the adoption of a commodity standard.

With the material provided by the authoritative and official pronouncements constituting Appendices I and II to this volume, readers will be able themselves to decide whether Sir Josiah Stamp's interpretation of the policy they proclaim, as expressed in the two quotations just given, or my interpretation, as expressed in the following chapters, is the more likely to mislead the President and the people of the United States.

My thanks are particularly due to the Committee for the Nation for supplying me with currency literature, without which Chapters V and VII could never have been written. I am also under great obligations to the currency writings of Messrs. Irving, Fisher, Keynes, Hawtrey, Robertson, and Mr. and Mrs. Cole, though perhaps none of them would recognise their opinions in the guise with which I have clothed them.

In view of certain criticisms of my previous book, I wish to state that, apart from the authorities quoted, I am expressing my own opinions. I make no claim to speak for any school of thought, or for any organised or authoritative body of opinion. I have interpreted certain authoritative and official documents and utterances which seemed to require interpretation, to the best of my ability. Whether I have overrated their importance or misread their significance may be left to the judgment of my readers.

C. M.-W.

January, 1935

TEN YEARS OF CURRENCY REVOLUTION

CHAPTER I

THE HISTORICAL APPROACH

" A study of history would, we believe, confirm the opinion
that it is in the changes in the level of prices, and in the
consequential alteration in the position of debtors and
creditors and the tax-gatherer, that the main secret of social
trouble is to be found."—Macmillan Report.

MONEY has a dominating influence upon our lives as
individuals. Our industrial activities are undertaken
to supply us with money with which to supply our
families with the means of livelihood. Our standard
of living is dictated by the money we earn, or receive
from other sources. Our social life is limited by the
amount of money we have to spare after bare necessities have been satisfied.

So it is with nations and empires. Money has a
dominating influence on the lives of communities. The
history of the world is a record of the fleeting existence
of kingdoms, empires, and civilisations. The extra-
ordinary influence which monetary problems have
exercised over every nation in the world since the war,
suggests that they exercised an equally potent influence
on the rise and decline of the communities which have
passed away. The records available are scanty. The

investigations of economic historians have scarcely begun. But it is possible to affirm that monetary influences were as powerful in the ancient world as they are to-day.

Indeed, they were more powerful. The invention of paper money has saved the world from the drastic currency deflations to which it was subject when it was dependent solely on metallic money. It was never possible in the ancient world to adjust the supply of the precious metals available for currency to the commercial demand. Either the currency was denuded by the abstraction of large quantities of gold and silver for the purposes of ostentation or display, or the nation expanded beyond the capacity of the metallic currency required to keep its commerce and industry alive. In either case, there was a severe currency deflation which ended in disruption and disaster. The short lived Kingdom of Israel and the Persian Empire are examples of disruption owing to the former cause. The Roman Empire is an example of a decline and fall owing largely to the latter cause.

Fortunately, there is a wealth of economic detail concerning the Kingdom of Israel in the record of the Books of Kings and Chronicles of the Biblical narrative. Founded by the warrior king, Saul, it rose to eminence owing to the administrative genius of his successor, David, who utilised its position at the centre of the trade routes of the world to raise it to eminence and prosperity. The third member of the dynasty, Solomon, did not include a knowledge of elementary economics in the great wisdom with which he was accredited, and speedily reduced the kingdom to beggary by denuding it of its gold, its international currency medium, and its silver, which provided its internal currency. To the economist, the reign of Solomon affords a study in rapid and concentrated currency deflation. Not content with his father's injunction to build the Temple, he built a larger, costlier and more sumptuous royal palace, and absorbed large amounts of gold and silver from the currency for its construction, furnishing and equipment. He wasted the precious metals extravagantly on his expensive marriages with foreign princesses, on the maintenance of his colossal household, and on an Oriental splendour and ostentation that excited the envy of the world. As an instance of the ruthless and misdirected deflation to which the currency was subjected, the records state that two hundred targets, each containing six hundred shekels of gold, and three hundred shields, each containing three pounds of gold, were constructed. No international currency could stand such wholesale diversions of its substance to non-commercial purposes. The international commerce with Egypt, Ophir, Sheba, Arabia, Assyria and Tyre and Sidon dwindled rapidly, and had vanished when Solomon died, a prey to disillusion and remorse.

The internal currency was deflated with equal recklessness. The provinces were so denuded of currency that it is recorded that "the king made silver to be in Jerusalem as stones." Jerusalem became a parasitic city living in luxury on the silver abstracted from the internal currency of the more remote parts of the kingdom.

The quotation from the Macmillan Report at the head of this chapter mentions the tax-gatherer as one of the causes of social revolt. The revolt of Jeroboam was more than a protest against heavy taxation. Taxation in the reign of Solomon meant not only taxation but also the denudation of the currency. It was doubly oppressive. The proceeds of modern taxation flow out of the Treasury back into circulation as soon as they are received. The proceeds of Solomon's taxation, except the small proportion paid to luxury workers and to Court and household officials, never went back into circulation. The currency received from taxation, being metallic, was retained for the most part for ostentation, and was permanently lost to the currency, national and international. The rebellion of the ten tribes was the result of the distress due, not only to taxation levied, but also to the loss of their currency. The loyalty of the two faithful tribes was the loyalty of parasites, the gratitude of the recipients of the extravagant expenditure of the Royal Court and household.

The heavy oppression of taxation in the ancient world was due to its deflative effect on the currency more than to its direct effect on the wealth of the people. The metals used for currency captured the imagination and excited the cupidity of the ruling powers, and a large proportion of the proceeds of taxation was retained for purposes of display. The deflative effect was cumulative. The longer a nation existed the greater was the accumulation of treasures at the Court, and the more the currency was depleted. The Persian Empire endured for centuries the routine abstraction of a large proportion of the currency received from the taxation levied, to add to the Royal treasures. The progressive deflation of the currency produced a gradual strangulation of the commerce on which the Empire had been founded. The power of resistance to outside aggression declined, as commerce and wealth declined, and Persia fell an easy prey to Alexander the Great in his endeavour to extend his dominion over Asia.

So great were the Persian treasures released by Alexander that they provided currency sufficient to create a remarkable expansion of commerce on the shores of the Mediterranean. Egypt, Phoenicia, Greece, Rome and Carthage, all felt the stimulus, which was similar in its operation to that subsequently provided by the release of the Peruvian and Mexican treasures after the discovery of America in the sixteenth century. Rome was the nation most able to take advantage of this literally golden opportunity, and gradually extended her supremacy over her rivals.

The supply of the precious metals provided a currency sufficient to finance the commerce of Rome till the time of Augustus. But the pay of the mercenaries in the border provinces of the Empire caused a severe drain on the currency resources of the capital. Most of this money never returned. It was either hoarded or absorbed in the local currencies of the remote provinces. A slow but steady deflation gradually diminished the currency required to finance the commerce of the Mediterranean and to supply the requirements of Rome itself. The growth of luxury in Rome stimulated the purchase of goods from distant parts of the Empire. The Balance of Trade between Rome and its provinces was invariably against Rome, with imports always exceeding its exports. This unfavourable balance of trade caused a steady flow of payments of currency from Rome to the provinces, and though this was modified to some extent by taxation and tribute, on the whole the movement of currency was in an outward direction. This movement continued from year to year and from century to century. The currency had dropped to less than one-tenth of its original volume by the eighth century A.D. The resulting decay of wealth and commerce was a potent contributory to the weakness of central control which led to the dissolution of the Empire.

The output of gold and silver from the mines of the world was insufficient to maintain commerce and civilisation in an expanded world at the high level they had reached in the palmy days of Egypt, Greece and Rome. The Dark Ages followed. Literature, Science and the Arts, as well as travel and international activity, are dependent on an active commerce. In the absence of an adequate currency, commerce languished, and national and international activity languished with it.

This prolonged halt in the progress of mankind must undoubtedly be associated with the relative scarcity of the precious metals, and the consequent shortage of the currency needed to finance commerce and civilisation. With equal certainty, the revival of all branches of national and international activity in Western Europe in the sixteenth century must be associated with the large supplies of gold and silver following the discovery of America. The inflation of currency was so severe that prices rose threefold in about a century, from the accession of Elizabeth (1558) to the Restoration of Charles (1660).

Britain was then threatened with a deflation of currency similar to that which caused the decline and fall of the Roman Empire. The demand for currency for the growing trade with North and Central America, with the East and West Indies and with China, and for the numerous experiments in colonisation then being undertaken, caused a serious drain of silver from Britain. The general demand for currency was so great that it outstripped the increasing production of gold and silver under European supervision in Mexico and Peru.

The world was saved from the fate of Rome by two agencies, the development of banking and the use of paper money. Deflation was avoided. Gold and silver were supplemented as currencies by such monetary devices as bank notes, bills of exchange, exchequer bills and banker's credit. These devices were not new. But it was not till the eighteenth century that they were utilised on such a scale that they made a substantial addition to the currency in circulation. Their adoption on such a scale acted as if rich new sources of gold and silver had been discovered. They gave a powerful stimulus to industry and commerce. They saved the world from the disaster of deflation to which purely metallic currencies were liable.

But they created the possibility of an equally great evil, that of inflation. Inflation is quite possible with a purely metallic currency, the inflation of the sixteenth century being an example. But an inflation through the increased supplies of the precious metals is both limited and gradual. Additional supplies of gold or silver are produced slowly, in limited quantities, and filter but gradually into circulation through the channels of trade. Consequently, a metallic inflation of currency, though a powerful stimulus to commerce, is never dangerous.

On the other hand, an increase of paper money is not necessarily limited or gradual, like an increase of a metallic currency. It can be created in unlimited quantities and injected immediately into the currency. Moreover, it does not, like gold or silver, lose its inflative force by dissipation over the whole area of the commercial world. It concentrates in the locality of issue and inflates the currency therein with concentrated force. Paper money cured the evil of deflation inherent in metallic money by rendering the world susceptible to the much more seductive danger of inflation.

Experience gradually suggested the method by which both evils could be controlled. By linking the amount of paper money in circulation to the amount of the precious metals held in reserve, the advantages of both classes of currency could be secured. The paper super-structure supplied elasticity and the means of adjusting the volume of currency in circulation to the require-ments of industry and commerce. The metallic reserve supplied stability and a safeguard against inflation.

The temptation of inflation to a weak Government, or to a Government in a difficult emergency is, however, often too great to resist. The issue of paper money in unlimited quantities, or even in quantities dispropor-tionate to the transactions they will be required to finance, brings temporary relief at the price of ulti-mate disaster. The *assignats* of the French Revolu-tionary Government, the greenbacks of the American Civil War, and the inflations of some Governments on the continent of Europe after the Great War, may be cited as inflations of paper money, adopted as desperate remedies for desperate emergencies.

It may seem a far cry from Solomon's Temple to the ten-year Currency Revolution, 1922–32. But the currency disease, which disrupted the Kingdom of Israel, which made Persia an easy prey to the armies of Alexander, and which contributed materially to the decline and fall of the Roman Empire, is precisely the same disease as that which drove Britain off the gold standard in 1931, and which compelled her to initiate a new and revolutionary currency system at Ottawa in 1932. The disease of currency deflation is as ancient as commerce or civilisation, and is as modern as the Continental gold bloc of the present day.

The historical approach, which has here been adopted, is more suited to the reader who has made no deep study of the theory of currency. The theoretical approach has many pitfalls for the student or for the ordinary reader. Familiar terms are used with unfamiliar meanings. Technical terms tend to obscurity. The definitions and conceptions of one economist are not invariably accepted by other economists. The attempt to secure precision in the definitions employed creates an impression of artificiality, and of divorce from the actual transactions and realities of everyday life. The branch of economics devoted to the investigation of currency problems is particularly liable to these drawbacks.

On the other hand, the historical method of approach, though it cannot attain to the scientific rigour of the theoretical method, is much more easy of comprehension. It uses economic terms with their everyday significance. It deals with actual occurrences rather than with theoretical illustrations specially devised to demonstrate a particular theory. It illustrates in a vivid and graphic manner the influence of economic forces on the fortunes of nations and empires, and on the rise and fall of civilisations. It links together the modern and ancient worlds. It proves that our currency problems and difficulties are not purely attributable to paper money, or to the effects of the Great War. They are problems and difficulties as old as civilisation. It is possible to obtain a much clearer conception of the currency revolution of 1922–32 through a preliminary knowledge that it was an effort to control currency forces which in the past have destroyed kingdoms and empires and have caused civilisations to vanish from the face of the earth.

CHAPTER II

HOW BANKERS MAKE MONEY

"What is money in the United States? Money in the United States is not only a relatively small amount of cash, but we have primarily the bank deposits, which have been comprised of proceeds of loans redeposited in banks practically to the extent of 90 per cent of the loans. Or rather, this money has been created by the banks through their volition, not through the volition of Congress and not with any co-ordination of judgment as to how much money was required in this country."—Mr. J. H. RAND, Chairman, Remington–Rand, New York City.

THE terms "Inflation" and "Deflation" have been used in the preceding chapter without the formal ceremony of a definition. The rough-and-ready meanings—that Inflation means too much money, and that Deflation means too little money—have been assumed. The formulation of precise definitions in the study of monetary problems is misleading. It creates a spurious atmosphere of certainty and exactitude which is not justified by the elementary stage to which the practice of currency has arrived. Currency is a mystery, a craft, an art, rather than a science. It is a mixture of mathematics and psychology that has not yet been reduced to scientific precision. Only a few of the secrets of its operation have yet been revealed.

Exact definitions of the terms Inflation and Deflation with respect to currency cannot possibly be given, except with reference to some ideal quantity of money required to produce the best results on the welfare of a nation. The conceptions of "too much money" and "too little money" have no definite meaning except with reference to some standard or right quantity of money. Economists are very much at variance as to how that right quantity of money should be described, or defined, or calculated. They are not even agreed as to the currency objectives which will produce the maximum of welfare in any community. Consequently Inflation and Deflation mean different things in the minds of different economists. One of the by-products of the World Economic Conference of 1933 was an excellent description of the objectives by which the equilibrium or stabilisation point of the new British currency policy should be determined. With the help of that description it may be possible to formulate exact definitions of the terms Inflation and Deflation. The subject is considered at greater length in Chapter XI.

Definitions cannot be more than tentative until bankers, financiers and economists have a much clearer conception of the meanings of the terms they use. At present there is no general agreement as to the exact meanings of such well-used terms as "capital," "investments," "profits" and "savings." The criticisms of Hawtrey and Robertson on Keynes' *Treatise on Money* centred very much round the validity of the definitions he adopted. Though the three economists are very much in sympathy in their conceptions of currency, they are at variance as to the appropriateness of each other's definitions.

Strangely enough, economists have not arrived at complete agreement as to the definition of the basis of all currency theory—money itself. In a recent essay on "The Demand for Money," by Professor Carver, published in the *Economic Journal* for June 1934, the following passage occurs:

This brings out an important difference between paper currency and that which is sometimes miscalled "bank money," but which should be called "bank credit," or better still, "bank cheques." This so-called "bank money" is not accepted freely from every one in payments to the Government, it is not legal tender for the payment of debts, and it has not yet become customary to accept it without a personal guarantee or endorsement in the purchase of commodities. The sole element in the desirability of this so-called "bank money" is its convertibility, or more accurately, the ability of the holder to get currency for it. The instant it loses its convertibility or its redeemability in currency, it loses all, or practically all, of its desirability and becomes worthless as a medium of exchange. The demand for commodities does not constitute a demand for this so-called money.

In this passage, the opinion that "bank money" is not money is expressed by the use of quotation marks every time it is mentioned, by the epithet "mis-called," and the thrice-repeated epithet "so-called." This opinion may be compared with the contrary opinion of Mr. Rand forming the introduction to this chapter. Professor Carver has achieved the paradox of being extreme in his orthodoxy. The weight of authority is against him. Keynes expresses the true nature of bank money in the two passages:

But the tendency is towards a preponderance of Bank Money, which in such countries as Great Britain and the United States constitutes perhaps nine-tenths of the aggregate of Current Money, and towards State Money occupying a definite subsidiary position.

and

If we include time deposits we find that State Money held by the public is less than 10 per cent of current money.

The Macmillan Report is equally definite against Professor Carver's contention, in the statement:

Actually in the modern world gold plays in the main only an indirect rôle in the determination of the price level, because the circulating media consist overwhelmingly of paper money and bank deposits.

The creation of bank money and its use as currency was in issue before the House of Representatives Sub-Committee on Banking and Currency when considering the Federal Monetary Authority Bill in January 1934. The following brief passage between Mr. F. W. Hancock, Member of the House of Representatives for North Carolina, and a Member of the Sub-Committee, and Professor Novick of New York University, is brief and to the point:

Mr. HANCOCK: Isn't it a fact that under the present-day banking system every private banker is issuing currency every day?

Professor NOVICK: You mean he is issuing circulation media which are the equivalent of currency? Yes.

The central fallacy of Professor Carver's contention is contained in the sentence:

The sole element in the desirability of this so-called "bank money" is its convertibility, or more accurately, the ability of the holder to get currency for it.

Here he confuses "convertibility" with reliability, a very different quality. Ninety per cent of the holders of cheques, or bank money, have no intention of getting currency for them. They place them to their own bank accounts and do not cash them. The classes of cheques which are converted into cash are very limited—those drawn for the payment of wages, those paid to persons who have no banking accounts, and those drawn to provide supplies of pocket money. Bank money as a whole is not convertible. It exists in virtue of the fact that only approximately 10 per cent of it will be required to be converted. It is one-tenth convertible and nine-tenths inconvertible. The test of a good cheque is not whether it is convertible, but whether it will be honoured. The statement that the sole element in the desirability of bank money is its convertibility is an irresponsible perversion of language. It has many elements of desirability. It is the most generally convenient form of money; it is particularly useful for making payments at a distance; it is habitually accepted as payment in the financial, industrial and commercial worlds; it is accepted by Government in settlement of its dues; it is accepted by tradesmen in payment of accounts; and, finally, it is safeguarded against abuse by elaborate provisions of the law.

Professor Carver's contention would wipe out

90 per cent of the world's currency. It would transform every modern work on currency into unmeaning gibberish. A true conception of bank money is essential to a clear understanding of the Currency Revolution that lasted for ten years, from 1922 to 1932. Bank money is a by-product of banking activities. Without intending to do so, every time a bank makes a loan, or purchases a security, it creates money. Many bankers to this very day deny that they do any such thing. They claim that they only lend money deposited into their charge by the public, and that for every loan they make they have a corresponding value of deposits.

Nevertheless, it is a fact that they do create money. The exposition of the method by which bankers make money is usually made in such technical language that it eludes the comprehension of the ordinary reader. It is worth an attempt to put it into comparatively simple language. When a bank makes a loan of £1,000, it does not ask itself the question—Have we £1,000 in hand to lend? Having satisfied itself of the solvency of the borrower, and of his security for repayment, it asks itself three questions:

i. Have we sufficient till money to cash any cheques that may be presented for cash payment?
ii. Have we sufficient reserves with the Bank of England to settle any adverse balance of cheques drawn upon us against cheques received by us?
iii. Are our loans and investments sufficiently liquid to be readily turned into cash, should an emergency arise?

Having answered these questions satisfactorily, it creates a paper account for the borrower out of nothing, and then authorises the borrower to draw on this account, created out of nothing, to the extent of £1,000. So far, bank money to the extent of £1,000 has been created but not put into circulation. The borrower puts the bank money so created into circulation, when he draws cheques for £1,000 against this unsubstantial account.

The bank has created the money out of its experience that on an average it will only have to cash about £60 worth of the cheques out of the total £1,000 drawn by the borrower. It will, in addition, have to provide about £50 from its reserves with the Bank of England to cover those of his cheques that may not be balanced by cheques received from other clients (Macmillan Report, paragraph 77). Experience has demonstrated that in normal times the remaining cheques for £890 drawn against the account are balanced by an equal value of cheques received. Thus, a bank can go on creating bank money so long as its till money is adequate to meet the small number of cheques presented for payment, its reserves at the Bank of England are adequate to meet its daily settlements, and its loans and investments are in a reasonably liquid condition.

It is the balancing figure of £890 that the bankers are thinking of when they claim that they do not advance money beyond their deposits. They contend that against the loan of £1,000 they make, they have £1,000 worth of assets—£60 till money, £50 reserve at the

Bank of England, and £890 deposits coming in from other sources. But this £890 is bank money artificially created out of nothing, exactly as the £1,000 loan was created out of nothing. Practice and experience has demonstrated that for every £100 held in cash and in reserves at the Bank of England, a commercial bank can create about £900 worth of bank money in addition.

In order that the above description may be supported by actual figures, the following statement, selected at random from the daily average of the banking returns for the month of December 1930, is herewith given. The returns for any day, or any month, of any year would give similar proportions.

			£
Banks' Cash in Hand	..	.. ..	103,880,000
Banks' reserves at Bank of England ..		..	78,362,000
Total cash and reserves	..	.. ..	182,242,000
Total Bank Money ..	..	.. ..	1,717,010,000

Thus, on a basis of £182,242,000, cash and reserves, the banks had created out of nothing but their experience and their credit a superstructure of £1,717,010,000 of bank money.

It is hoped that the above explanation of how bankers create money is stated in sufficiently clear language to be readily understood. The explanation is usually made incomprehensible to the ordinary reader by the statement that the bank creates deposits, and then issues loans against the deposits so created. The ordinary reader usually gives up in despair on coming to such a statement. He finds himself up against the following difficulties:

    i. Deposits are money placed into a bank by the public; how can they be created by the bankers?

    ii. Deposits are something deposited; how can they be created out of nothing?

    iii. How can a banker make a deposit with himself?

    iv. A deposit is something fixed, immovable, stationary, locked up in a bank; why do economists talk of deposits as being bank money, mobile, circulating, and passing from hand to hand?

    v. How can the purchase of a security by a bank create money?

    vi. How can a bank allow ten times more cheques to circulate than it can pay in cash?

The following replies are an attempt to explain the above paradoxes:

    i. Only a small proportion of the deposits are placed in the banks by the public; the greater proportion are created in the manner explained in the next reply.

    ii. A bank creates a deposit out of nothing, by opening an account for a borrower, with no money passing between them, and then allowing the borrower to treat this imaginary account as if it were a deposit. The deposit is used by the customer but it has been created by the banker.

    iii. Having created the money out of his imagination, the banker enters it in his books as a deposit with himself to enable the borrower to draw cheques upon it.

    iv. It is misleading to talk of deposits as currency. It is the cheques which are the currency. The term "deposits" is used for currency merely in a statistical sense. The total deposits form the limit up to which cheques can be drawn, and it is convenient to use the figure for the total deposits as representing the total of cheques in circulation, or the total of bank money.

v. When a bank buys a security, it does not ask itself the question whether it has the money to pay for it; it asks the same three questions about its cash, its reserves and its liquidity as it asks when it makes a loan. If the answers are satisfactory, it buys the security with a cheque. The cheque will not (in nine cases out of ten) be cashed, but will be placed by the seller of the security to his banking account. Thus, the total amount of deposits or of bank money will be increased by this addition to the seller's deposits at his bank. The bank, by its issue of the cheque which purchased the security, has created additional bank money to that amount.

vi. Banks can allow cheques to circulate to an extent of ten times their cash and reserves, because the majority of cheques are never presented for payment. They are paid into banking accounts. The banks have a machinery called clearing by which these cheques are balanced against each other, and only the differences settled between them. The figures given above demonstrate that for a daily average of cheques issued to the extent of £1,717 millions, in December 1930, a sum of £103 millions of cash was sufficient to pay all that were presented for cash payment, and a reserve of £78 millions was sufficient to settle all clearing balances.

The creation of so large a proportion of the currency required for the purpose of industry and commerce by the banking system is the cause of the large and increasing volume of criticism directed against the banks and bankers. Such criticism is much more bitter in the United States than in Britain. The main heads of this criticism are:

i. The creation of bank money is an encroachment by the banking system on the prerogative of the

State. The State should be solely responsible for the supply of money required by the community, and should not rely on any outside factor to undertake its responsibilities and carry out its duties.

ii. The banking system charges interest for the bank money it creates; the community, and industry and commerce, are entitled to an adequate supply of money to carry out the normal transactions of the everyday life of the country, free from the obligation to pay interest for it.

iii. The interest charged by the banking system is really based on the credit of the community. It is not equitable for the public to pay, and for the banks to receive, interest based on public credit.

iv. The banking system, however impartial it may be, is bound to give prior consideration to its own needs and to the requirements of finance, rather than to the needs of commerce and industry. (The working of the gold standard is an illustration of this tendency.)

v. The banking system gives preferential treatment and preferential rates of interest to international commerce and finance, at the expense of internal trade and industry. Call money and short-term money at rates round about 2 per cent is at the disposal of international commerce and finance; whereas a minimum of 5 per cent is charged for accommodation to manufacturers and merchants catering for home industry.

vi. The Trade Cycle is due to the mismanagement (partly deliberate, partly inefficient) of the supply of bank money to the community by the banking system.

vii. The existence of poverty in a world of plenty is due to the banking system regulating its supply of bank money on obsolete principles.

viii. The world depression of the last ten years has been due to the fact that the banking system has not been able to adapt the supply of bank money to the requirements of a post-war world.

34

Without attempting to justify or rebut these criticisms, it may be explained that the creation of bankers' money is an unconscious development of banking. Neither Government, nor the public, nor economists, nor the bankers themselves, for a long time, had the faintest conception that when they issued loans, or purchased securities, they were creating money. When some daring economist first exposed the truth he was received with a storm of indignant protests and denials. The quotation from Professor Carver, earlier in this chapter, demonstrates that even now the fact of the creation of bank money by bankers is not universally accepted.[1]

The unconscious growth and the very gradual acceptance of the fact that bankers can, and do, create money explains how this encroachment on the prerogative of Government was allowed to proceed without challenge. When it became more generally known, it was concealed from the public by the fiction that the operation of the gold standard was automatic, and that any interference with its automatic working would produce unmentionable disasters. Moreover, the more gross abuses of the bankers' practice of creating money were not developed till after the war. They did not become unendurable until it was perceived that the banking system was hopelessly unable to cope with the post-war problems of commerce and industry. Further aspects of this question are subsequently

[1] In order to combat the demand for Government control of the Bank of England, *The Times* has recently strongly supported the denial of the fact that banks create money, both in its City articles and in its Annual Financial Review (12/2/35).

discussed in Chapters IV, IX, and XI. Anticipating a little, it may here be stated that a very elementary attempt to bring the creation of bank money more under public control was made at the Ottawa Conference in 1932, and confirmed and expanded by the British Empire Currency Declaration in 1933.

It is impossible to understand the Currency Revolution extending from 1922 to 1932 without a clear understanding of the nature and importance of bank money. It was a curtailment of bank money which caused the severe depressions of industry in Britain and the United States in 1921. It was the judicious control of bank money by Governor Strong which was the principal feature of the American Currency Revolution of 1922, which in turn carried the United States to the highest pitch of prosperity it had ever experienced. It was the injudicious curtailment of bank money, resulting from the return to a gold standard in 1925, which caused the depression of British industry from 1925 to 1931. It was the distrust of bank money on the Continent of Europe, resulting in the hoarding epidemic, which drove Britain off the gold standard in 1931. It was the unwise inflation of bank money which caused the American collapse in 1929. And finally, it is the belief that the judicious regulation of bank money can restore remunerative prices, and give stability to the purchasing power of money, that is the foundation of the existing system of international currency established by the Currency Revolution effected at Ottawa in 1932.

CHAPTER III

THE METALLIC COMPLEX

"So long as people have confidence, they are not going to call for redemption, but when confidence flees and people begin to get frightened, and realise that we have not gold with which to redeem, they rush for redemption, as happened when we went off the gold standard. Confidence was shaken. If we had a sufficient metallic base to redeem, confidence would not flee, and we would need only that to hold confidence. Whenever confidence disappears the crash comes. But, as I have said, if we had sufficient redemption metal to take care of everybody, and everybody knew it, fear would not come and the crash would not come."—Mr. O. H. CROSS, Member of the U.S. House of Representatives for Texas.

THE people of Britain have one supreme currency virtue. They are not victims of the metallic complex. The currency psychology of the people of the United States in a time of financial crisis, so vividly portrayed by Mr. Cross in the above quotation, is worlds apart from British psychology in similar circumstances. British currency problems are free from the numerous metallic issues which have so hampered and complicated President Roosevelt's efforts towards reform.

To British minds, such matters as the price of gold, the gold content of the pound, the convertibility of the pound, the internal hoarding of gold, and the monetisation of silver, appear as irrelevant side issues, distracting attention from the central relevant problem. Had the Ottawa delegates, in 1932, been deflected from their purpose by such issues, nothing would have been accomplished.

Gold and silver have never been regarded, in Britain, with feelings of exaggerated respect or reverence. Their worth has been estimated from a purely utilitarian standpoint. They have qualities which render them ideal currency media for primitive, stationary or unprogressive countries. They are durable, pleasant to the eye, intrinsically valuable, universally acceptable, fairly stable in value, and have an age-long tradition of superstition and utility as currency metals behind them.

But they have grave defects, rendering them quite unfit to provide, unaided, the currency of advanced or progressive commercial countries. They are costly to transport, inconvenient and dangerous to carry about in large quantities, intolerably bulky for large payments, and unsuitable for making payments at a distance. Moreover, as commerce and industry advance, forces are engendered which deprive them of their stability of value. Unless placed under rigorous control and continuous management they fluctuate in purchasing power widely and rapidly.

But their gravest defect is the impossibility of regulating their supply to meet the needs of a country, or a world, continuously progressing in industrial and commercial development. The production and supply of gold and silver cannot be co-ordinated with the world's demands for currency. The Roman Empire declined and fell largely because the world supplies of gold and silver were not able to supply its commercial requirements. The world stagnated in the Dark Ages because of an insufficiency of the precious metals. The modern world requires a supply of currency far beyond the capacity of gold and silver to provide. It has been saved from the fate of Rome by supplementing gold and silver by various forms of paper money, which now perform by far the greater volume of currency transactions.

Another grave defect of gold and silver as currency media is the conflict they stimulate between the two recognised functions of money, the storage of savings and the medium of exchange. In a primitive or stationary community these two functions can usually be performed without encroaching on each other. But in the modern world, the use of money for the storage of savings, or hoarding, can only be accomplished at the expense of its other function, that of providing currency, or a medium of exchange. Hoarding on anything beyond a moderate scale causes a deflation of the currency. The outstanding instance is the hoarding on the continent of Europe in 1931, which caused so severe a deflation that it forced Britain to withdraw from the gold standard.

The force of tradition is so strong, and experience in the management of paper money is so limited, that the amount of paper money in circulation is usually regulated by the amount of gold and silver held in reserve. This has given these metals a fictitious and superstitious importance as being, in some special manner, the only true money. Their very defects, that they are incapable of performing the currency functions of the modern world, and require to be supplemented by another medium, have been twisted so as to appear as supreme virtues. The force of tradition behind them has drawn a sentimental veil over their deficiencies, and given rise to the superstition that paper money derives its value from their backing. Paper money, in actual fact, derives its value from its utility, its elasticity, its adaptability, its capacity to perform financial transactions completely beyond the range of gold and silver. But over the greater part of the world this truth is ignored, and gold and silver are revered as being the only real forms of money.

The freedom of Britain from this superstition is due to the influence of the pound sterling. The pound sterling is not a coin. It is a paper money of account. The dollar has always been regarded primarily as a coin, with a certain silver or gold content. But the pound, except for a period of sixty years (1544 to 1604) in the sixteenth century, has never been a coin. Even when, in 1816, Britain went on to a gold standard, although the pound sterling was made the unit of that standard, it was not allowed to degenerate into a coin. It was represented in the coinage by the golden sovereign, but itself remained an intangible money of account. A mere catalogue of the various forms assumed by the pound sterling in the course of its existence for nine hundred years, will explain how it has formed an integral part of English (and subsequently of British) history, and how it has continually adapted itself to the requirements of the period it served. It is given here because it illustrates the currency psychology of the British people, and how their loyalty to the pound sterling is due to its adaptability to the changing needs of progressive development.

Norman Period: A pound weight (troy) of silver pennies.

Plantagenet Period: A pound weight (troy) of silver coinage.

Fifteenth Century: A paper money of account of variable silver value.

Early Tudor Period: A paper money of account of the value of twenty silver shillings.

Elizabethan Period: A gold coin—the gold pound.

1604–1774: A paper money of account of the value of twenty silver shillings.

1774–97: A paper money of account, equated to gold in the ratio 20:21 of the guinea.

1797–1816: The unit of an inconvertible paper currency.

1816–1914: A unit of account, linked to gold by the fixed price £3 17s. 10½d. per ounce, and by a gold coin, the sovereign.

August–December 1914: The unit of an inconvertible paper currency.

1915–18: A paper money of account, linked to gold by means of a gold coin, the U.S. Dollar.

1919–April 1925: The unit of an inconvertible paper currency.

April 1925–September 1931: A unit of account, linked to gold by the fixed price of £3 17s. 10½d. per ounce, but of limited internal convertibility.

September 1931–August 1932: The unit of an inconvertible paper currency.

August 1932 to date: A managed unit of an inconvertible paper currency, based on the movement of the wholesale price level on a Price Index towards an equilibrium point, as yet undetermined.

The dominance which the pound sterling has achieved in the British monetary system, and its influence throughout the world, is due to its comparative long-period stability as a money of account. A money of account is of far greater importance than a coin. A transaction by means of a coin is momentary. A money of account is the only medium in which such transactions as loans, debts, bonds, securities, investments, contracts, mortgages, cheques, bills of exchange, price lists (offers to sell), credits and instalments can be recorded. It continues from day to day, from year to year and from century to century. It links the present with the past and with the future. It was a stable money of account that President Roosevelt desired when he stated that "the United States seeks the kind of a dollar which a generation hence will have the same purchasing and debt-paying power as the dollar value we hope to attain in the near future."

Sir Henry Strakosch, in his memorandum of evidence to the Macmillan Commission, thus described a money of account:

In our complex economic organisation, the vast majority of transactions are not settled when they are concluded, but they almost always involve contracts expressed in money amounts, the settlement of which is deferred over widely varying periods.

British indifference to the metallic substance of its money is largely due to the fact that the pound sterling, as a money of account, was not, except for a brief period, a coin. It was illustrated by the nonchalance with which the standard silver currency was allowed to drain away in the eighteenth century. The same indifference was apparent when cash payments were suspended in 1797 owing to the heavy drain of gold for the Napoleonic Wars. The paper pound was accepted as readily as the golden guinea had been accepted when the silver coinage drained away. With a debased silver currency and a vanished guinea, the paper pound was accepted as a common sense and workable solution of a difficult monetary problem.

Smart, in his *Economic Annals of the Nineteenth Century* states:

> The London merchants held a meeting at the Mansion House and passed a unanimous resolution declaring that they would not refuse to receive Bank Notes in payment of any sums of money to be paid to them, and would use their utmost endeavours to make all their payments in the same manner.

Cobbett, in his *Rural Rides,* gives an even more graphic description of the perfect freedom of the British people from the metallic complex even as long ago as the end of the eighteenth century. He records:

> With what eagerness in 1797 did the nobility and gentry and clergy rush forward to give their sanction and their support to the new system which then began. They assembled in all the counties and put forth declarations that they would take the paper of the Bank.

There was none of the resentment which was aroused at a much later date by the issue of the "greenbacks" in the emergency caused by the American Civil War. Inflation there was, of course. A continental war of twenty-five years' duration, involving heavy subsidies from Britain to her allies, could not be waged without some degree of inflation. But the inflation never got out of hand. The daily temptation to inflate the currency by printing paper money to meet their pressing requirements was resisted by the British Government. The paper pound fell below its gold value. But it never fell below recovery. Six years only, after the conclusion of the Napoleonic Wars, were sufficient to restore the paper pound to gold parity and to provide sufficient sovereigns to meet the needs of the internal circulation.

The restraint adopted by the British Government from 1797 to 1816, was repeated again during the two periods of inconvertibility, 1919 to 1925, and 1931 to date, after the departure of Britain from the gold standard. The method by which Britain has, on these occasions, enabled an inconvertible paper currency to operate as efficiently as a currency based on gold has been described by Dr. Sprague in the words:

If you will act in running the monetary system practically as you would act if you were on the gold, you can get virtually all the advantages of being on gold. . . . The danger is that countries would not do that (Appendix IV).

This evidence is a remarkable tribute to British capacity for currency management. It acknowledges that Britain is so free from the metallic complex that it has the aptitude to operate its currency on correct lines, whether on a gold standard or not. It also suggests that other countries have not that aptitude. Dr. Sprague's

44

evidence to this effect was received with such astonishment and incredulity that it led to the following remarkable question, and equally remarkable answer:

Mr. CROSS: If they [the British] had no gold, and there was no probability of their ever going back to the gold standard, and if they knew there was no chance of doing that, and that they would always have inconvertible paper, do you not think it would have a terrific effect on them?

Dr. SPRAGUE: It would have an effect which could, I think, be overcome gradually, and perhaps speedily, if the world were convinced that the British Government would go forward on virtually the same line that it followed during the last two years. One does not know how the pound will be revalued when the world goes back to gold, but there is very great confidence in the pound sterling.

The whole passage can be studied in full in Appendix IV, but the above question and answer are so directly relevant to the theme of this chapter that they are worthy of special quotation. Dr. Sprague's reply, in effect, is that Britain's currency policy is so independent of gold that in a very short space of time she would be quite capable of managing an international currency without any gold whatever.

A more detailed and systematic reply to the queries in Mr. Cross's question would be:

i. Britain will always be able to purchase as much gold as she requires for currency purposes, by paying the market price for it.
ii. There is no probability of Britain's return to the gold standard. A return to the pre-war gold standard is impossible. A return to the gold standard of 1925 to 1931 would be disastrous. A return to a gold standard, as recommended by the Genoa Conference,

has been rendered impossible by the revival of the primitive practice of hoarding; and, in any case, would be but a poor variant of the Ottawa Currency Policy. A return to some fancy and unfamiliar form of the gold standard would be bitterly opposed by Australia and New Zealand, and by the whole of the Industrial and Labour forces of Britain.

iii. Britain is perfectly satisfied with an inconvertible internal currency, and can provide all the gold needed for her international transactions by purchasing it at market price.

iv. Instead of having a terrific effect, the knowledge that Britain's internal currency will always be inconvertible is a matter of complete indifference and unconcern to the British Public.

The British attitude to gold is that of a nation of shopkeepers. A shopkeeper would not agree with the economists' dictum that one of the functions of money is to provide a store for savings. A shopkeeper puts his savings back into his business, into his stock, into his shop-window. He regards hoarding as a perversion of money from its proper use, a wicked waste of a good asset. Even when a Briton is prevented by untoward circumstances from following the national occupation of keeping a shop, he never dreams of storing his savings in money. He has invented a multitudinous series of facilities and associations for storing his savings, the most familiar being Investment, Insurance, Bank Deposits, Friendly Societies, Co-operative Societies, Building Societies and Savings Banks. The hoarding of money is so exceptional that it is regarded as being a sure sign of eccentricity and abnormality.

It is interesting to compare the British attitude on

the occasion of the withdrawal from the gold standard in 1931 with that of the people of the United States when that nation withdrew from gold in 1933. According to the statement of Mr. Cross at the head of this chapter, the people of the United States got frightened, lost confidence, and rushed for redemption. Although there was approximately £1,000,000,000 worth of gold in the Federal Reserve Banks at the time, there was a panic run on the banks, which spread from bank to bank until it threatened the whole banking system with disaster.

On the other hand, with the reserve of the Bank of England reduced to its last sovereign (see Appendix IV), there was not the faintest thought or apprehension of a panic in Britain in 1931. Nobody rushed to the banks for redemption. A feeling of indescribable relief as from an intolerable burden pervaded the country. Instead of a rush to try to obtain gold, there was a rush in the opposite direction. Everybody tried to convert every bit of gold they happened to have by them into inconvertible paper money. Desks, drawers and bureaux were ransacked to see if some odd sovereign had been overlooked, or if there were any old and forgotten trinkets that could be sold at a moderate profit and turned into paper money. Afternoon whist and bridge parties were held up while the players related to each other with glee stories of the unexpected windfalls they had obtained by disposing of any odd coins or bits of golden jewellery they had unexpectedly found in their possession.

In one respect the British indifference to gold

amounted to a positive danger. They have always under-rated the foreign passion for gold, and have never kept enough gold in reserve to provide a sufficient margin for safety in proportion to the immense volume of international liabilities they have assumed. There were banking crises in 1825, 1847, 1857 and 1866, all due to the fact that the Bank of England and the London Money Market were undertaking vast commitments on an absurdly small gold reserve. Both the Bank of England and the banks and merchant houses comprising the London Money Market have always relied upon their capacity for currency and financial management rather than upon adequate gold reserves to pull them through tight places.

Foreign economists and financiers have frequently expressed their astonishment at what they regard as the serious disproportion between Britain's gold reserves and her international liabilities. In 1929 Britain had greater international commitments than either France or the United States, yet the gold reserves of Britain were £146 millions as compared with £336 millions held by France and £802 millions held by the United States. The disparity grew greater month by month, yet in March 1930 Mr. Montagu Norman was quite confident that the British gold reserves were both adequate and safe, as the following passage from his evidence to the Macmillan Commission will indicate:

Lord MACMILLAN: If that instrument [the bank rate] is used for the purpose of preserving the stock of gold, is it effective for that purpose?

Mr. MONTAGU NORMAN: It is effective.
Lord MACMILLAN: How far is the instrument with which
you are equipped effective for the purpose?
Mr. MONTAGU NORMAN: It is effective.
Lord MACMILLAN: For that purpose?
Mr. MONTAGU NORMAN: It is effective in my opinion.

That evidence was given just twelve months before
the serious drain on the Bank of England's stock of
gold began, and about eighteen months before that
drain forced Britain off the gold standard.

Notwithstanding Mr. Norman's evidence, the Macmillan Report considered that the Bank of England's
gold reserves were too low, and repeatedly recommended that they should be strengthened as follows:

We recommend that the Bank's normal holdings of gold,
or its equivalent in foreign exchange, should, in view of the
large liability of London as an international banking centre,
be larger than they have been in recent years.

Also:

The Bank of England's liquid assets ought to be increased
at the first opportunity to a substantially higher figure, and
maintained thereafter at this higher figure as the normal.

And:

The magnitude of London's international operations
to-day requires that the normal level of the Bank of England's
liquid international assets should be materially higher than
it now is.

Finally:

It would seem advisable for the Bank to supplement its
gold reserves by liquid funds held abroad.

It is clear that the British attitude of indifference to
gold led to a dangerous under-estimation of the quantity

of gold reserves required to perform international banking and currency functions for a world with a much more decided passion for gold than that possessed by Britain.

In another direction, Britain's indifference to gold saved the world from disaster. The early operations of the gold standard adopted by Britain led to a drain of the world's gold to Britain. One of the objects of the adoption of Free Trade by Britain was to save the debtor nations from bankruptcy owing to the loss of their gold under the operation of the gold standard. Britain's policy, due to her detachment from gold, resulted in an equitable distribution of gold throughout the world for seventy years prior to the Great War. Since the power to control the distribution of gold was lost by Britain, its maldistribution has been one of the causes of the depressions and disasters that have oppressed the world since the war.

Britain was driven from the gold standard in 1931 by the strength of the metallic complex on the continent of Europe, and by her under-estimate of the strength of that complex. The hoarding price of gold defeated the currency price of gold, and demonstrated the unfitness of gold to be the basis of an international currency. The primary consideration of the delegates at Ottawa in 1932 was to devise a new system of international currency which would be hoarding-proof. They took the following phrase from the Report of the Genoa Conference, held in 1922, ten years previously:

With a view to preventing undue fluctuations in the purchasing power of gold,

and deliberately modified it, while keeping closely to the original phrasing, so that it would read:

With a view to avoiding, so far as may be found practicable, wide fluctuations in the purchasing power of standards of value. (Appendix I.)

Some of the nations of the British Commonwealth are even more free from the metallic complex than Britain. It is doubtful whether Britain by herself, despite the lamentable failure of gold as a basis for currency in 1931, would have flouted gold quite so deliberately as the Ottawa delegates did in the concluding sentence of the Ottawa Monetary Report. But the delegates from Australia and New Zealand were not so sensitive. Hoarding had made gold susceptible to incalculable fluctuations in purchasing power. The whole financial strength of the Bank of England, resolutely backed by the Bank of France and the Federal Reserve Board of the United States, had proved powerless to control such fluctuations in 1931. Therefore gold should not be recommended as the future currency standard. It had been weighed in the balances and was found wanting. The Ottawa delegates had a very clear conception as to what the objectives of the future international currency standard should be. But they had such grave doubts as to whether they could be achieved by a gold standard, that they refused to assume the responsibility of recommending or forecasting a return to gold.

CHAPTER IV

THE GOLD STANDARD

".... the disastrous inefficiency which the international gold standard has worked since its restoration five years ago (fulfilling the worst fears and gloomiest prognostications of its opponents) and the economic losses, second only in amount to those of a great war, which it has brought upon the world. ...."—Mr. J. M. KEYNES.

THE system of currency, known as the gold standard, is an outstanding example of deliberate and effective currency management. It had its origin in an ambitious experiment in currency manipulation more than a century before its formal adoption in 1816. In the opening years of the eighteenth century, Britain was threatened with a drain on its standard currency, exactly similar to that which had caused the fall of the Roman Empire centuries earlier. The development of colonisation and the expanding trade with North and Central America, the East and West Indies, and China called for large quantities of currency, and a severe drain on the silver coinage of the kingdom set in. Under the direction of Sir Isaac Newton, the great mathematician and philosopher, Warden of the Mint, a series of most fascinating currency experiments was undertaken. The problem was to transfer the drain on currency from silver to gold. Silver was the standard currency, whereas gold was a luxury currency for the convenience of the wealthy and of the expanding trade of the merchants of London, and could more easily be spared. The principal gold coin was the guinea, originally issued to circulate at the value of twenty silver shillings. But it had never been issued in adequate quantities, and its scarcity caused it to appreciate in value, and in the year 1700 it was circulating at a value of thirty shillings.

As the market value of the guinea on the Continent at that time was about 21s., it was obviously impossible to pay British debts on the Continent with guineas. To pay a debt of 21s. with a coin circulating at 30s. was not a commercial proposition. Under Sir Isaac's advice, a proclamation was issued reducing the circulating value of the guinea from 30s. to 26s. He backed up the proclamation by issuing guineas in such numbers that their value depreciated to that fixed by proclamation.

He did not succeed in his objective. Silver coinage still continued to leave the country, and the guineas remained behind. But though he did not stop the drain of silver, he made two valuable discoveries: first, that it was a highly profitable transaction to buy gold at 21s. on the Continent and issue it as guineas worth 26s. for circulation; and secondly, that there was a strong demand in Britain for all the guineas and half-guineas that he could issue.

Fortified with this knowledge he made a second attempt. The guineas were reduced by proclamation to 22s., and more guineas were coined to bring them down to this level. And still gold refused to leave the country. The third experiment reduced the guinea to 21s. 6d., but met with the same result. The fourth, and most famous, of these experiments was made in 1717, after an exhaustive report by Sir Isaac on "The State of the Gold and Silver Coins of the Kingdom." The guinea was reduced to 21s. And still gold obstinately refused to leave the country, and the drain on the silver currency continued.

Sir Isaac was quite prepared to continue these experiments indefinitely until he had reduced the circulating value of the guinea to its market value on the Continent, and thereby rendered it capable of discharging external debts. But he retired, and his successor, Conduitt, perceived that gold was a more suitable metal for Britain's internal requirements than silver. The silver currency was allowed to drain away, and almost unconsciously the standard of currency was transferred from silver to gold.

By this series of experiments Sir Isaac Newton added to his important list of mathematical discoveries a further discovery of extreme importance to all future currency administration. He had discovered the quantity theory of money. That theory has since been elaborated from the crude form in which it had been discovered by the Newtonian currency experiments. But even in that crude form—that the purchasing power of money, or its circulating value, depended rather on the quantity in circulation than on the substance or metal in which it was embodied—it was destined to have a profound influence on monetary history and administration.

The first practical application of this theory was the stabilisation of the guinea at a rate of 21 : 20 to the unit of account, the pound sterling. Previous gold coins, the sovereign, the gold pound, the unite, the broad, and the guinea itself up to 1717 had never kept in step with the pound sterling. But for eighty years, from 1717 to 1797, the guinea was kept at the constant ratio of 21 : 20 with the pound, not by the method of proclamation, but by the method of currency manipulation. The issue of guineas was governed by the necessity of keeping this rate constant.

The quantity theory of money thus discovered by a series of practical currency experiments is the basis of all policies of currency management. The objective of all currency policies is to secure the stability of the circulating value of money, or of purchasing power, or of the general price level—all different methods of saying the same thing. Divergent currency policies are due to divergent conceptions of stability. In particular, the stability of the international exchanges, the primary objective of all gold standard systems, is merely an indirect method of securing the stability of the world price level. Also, the stability of the internal price level, or the internal purchasing power of money, is not necessarily the same as the stability of the world price level, or of the purchasing power of an international currency. Consequently, these two divergent stabilities may lead to conflicting currency policies.

The practical experience of the working of the quantity theory of money, gained in the stabilisation of the guinea from 1717 to 1797, was of inestimable value in the difficult years of the suspension of cash payments from 1797 to 1816. The same policy was pursued in printing paper money as had been pursued in coining golden guineas. Only sufficient notes were printed to meet legitimate currency requirements. In the words of Dr. Sprague (see Appendix IV), "if you will act in running the monetary system practically as you would act if you were on the gold, you can get virtually all of the advantages of being on gold." Even at the commencement of the nineteenth century Britain demonstrated that she could administer a stable currency quite independently of gold.

The adoption of a gold standard by Britain in 1816 was not due to any particular veneration or reverence felt towards gold as the basis of currency. Britain might be capable of maintaining a currency independently of gold, but owing to Britain's international position, the psychology of the rest of the world had to be taken into consideration. If the new British currency was to secure the confidence of the world, gold was the obvious basis to select. The selection was determined on purely utilitarian considerations. A stable basis of currency was required for both internal trade and external commerce. Gold was rightly selected as being the substance best fulfilling the requirements.

The adoption of a gold standard, with the sterling

price of £3 17s. 10½d. per ounce, as its unit value, called for far more rigorous and continuous measures of currency management than had ever previously been exercised. The price of gold had to be rigorously imprisoned between the narrow and rigid limits of £3 17s. 9d. and £3 17s. 10½d. per ounce. The immense and powerful forces of supply and demand, unceasingly operating to free gold from this position of captivity, had to be kept at bay. Day by day for ninety-two years (1822 to 1914) the vigilance of the Bank of England never relaxed. The financial power of the British Government, the whole weight of Britain's strong creditor position in the world, the immense volume of British international commerce, the large sums annually invested by Britain in the development of more backward countries, were all utilised in this elaborate scheme of currency management. Such management was concentrated on the one main objective, the stabilisation of the price of gold at the sterling figure.

The Macmillan Report specifies five methods at the disposal of the Bank of England for the management of the gold standard:

    i. The bank rate.
   ii. Open market operations (that is the purchase and sale of securities) undertaken to influence the amount of the reserves of the commercial banks, and their power of creating bankers' money.
  iii. Open market operations, undertaken to influence the London Money Market.
  iv. Gold exchange methods—dealings in foreign exchanges and in forward exchange, and variations in the price of gold within the narrow limits permitted.

    v. Personal influence or advice—such as the so-called embargo on foreign loans.

Of these methods, the manipulation of the bank rate is the most important. The other methods are subsidiary methods, usually undertaken to avoid the necessity of modifying the bank rate, or else to supplement the movement of the bank rate and assist it to attain the desired objective. The working of currency control was described by Horsley Palmer, the Governor of the Bank of England, in 1832, and again by the Cunliffe Currency Committee in 1918. The similarity of the two descriptions at an interval of eighty-six years is an eloquent testimony to the consistency and continuity of the currency management exercised by the Bank during that interval. Horsley Palmer explained the effect of curtailing currency and credit in the following terms:

> The first operation is to increase the value of money [N.B.—by the term "value of money" Horsley Palmer meant the short-term rate of interest]; with the increased value of money there is less facility obtained by the commercial public in the discount of their paper; that naturally tends to limit transactions and to the reduction of prices; the reduction of prices will so far alter our situation with foreign countries that it will be no longer an object to import, but the advantage will rather be upon the export; the gold and silver will then come back to the country and rectify the contraction that previously existed.

The description of the operation of raising the bank rate by the Cunliffe Report in 1918 gives the same results in more detail:

The raising of the Bank's discount rate, and the steps taken to make it effective in the market, necessarily led to a general rise in interest rates and a restriction of credit. New enterprises were therefore postponed, and the demand for constructional materials and other capital goods was lessened. The consequent slackening of employment also diminished the demand for consumable goods, while holders of stocks of commodities carried largely with borrowed money, being confronted with an increase of interest charges, if not with actual difficulty of renewing loans, and with the prospect of falling prices, tended to press their goods on a weak market. The result was a decline in general prices in the Home Market which, by checking imports, corrected the adverse trade balance, which was the primary cause of the difficulty.

In other words, the operations of currency management conferred upon the Bank of England the power to restrict credit, to postpone new enterprises, to lessen the demand for constructional materials and other capital goods, to create unemployment, to diminish the demand for consumable goods, to cause difficulty in renewing loans, to confront manufacturers with the prospect of falling prices, to force dealers to press their goods on a weak market, and to cause a decline in general prices on the home market. In brief, the stability of the international exchanges was accomplished by a process which deliberately caused universal depression in industry, created unemployment, and forced manufacturers to produce, and merchants to sell, at a loss.

The Cunliffe Report casts a revealing light on the six years of depression which Britain suffered under the gold standard regime from 1925 to 1931. In his evidence to the Macmillan Commission, Mr. Montagu Norman endeavoured to minimise the devastating effect on British industry, due to the high bank rate necessary for the maintenance of the gold standard. The following passage explains his attitude:

Lord MACMILLAN: You may be effecting an operation of great value from the financial point of view, which, nevertheless, has unfortunate repercussions internally by restricting credit and enterprise. Your instrument may be doing good in one direction and harm in another. I should like to have from you your conception of the internal effect of the alteration of the bank rate. Externally you say it achieves its purpose of arresting the flow of gold if you raise the bank rate. Internally, how do you conceive that it operates?

Mr. MONTAGU NORMAN: Well, I should think that its internal effect was as a rule greatly exaggerated—that its actual ill effects were greatly exaggerated, and that they are much more psychological than real.—Much more psychological than actual.

Lord MACMILLAN: But even if it has psychological consequences, they may be depressing consequences, and may be serious?

Mr. MONTAGU NORMAN: Yes, but not so serious as they are usually made out to be. . . . I think that the disadvantages to the internal position are relatively small compared with the advantages to the external position.

This cynical repudiation by the Governor of the Bank of England of the orthodox opinion of the operation of the bank rate and of the accounts of its operation given by his predecessors was too much for Mr. Keynes, who was a member of the Commission. He proceeded to put Mr. Norman through a severe cross-examination, and finally, after an exhibition of skilful fencing on both sides, succeeded in eliciting the following:

Mr. J. M. KEYNES: What I thought was the more or less accepted theory of the bank rate was that it works in two ways. It has the effect on the international situation that has been described to-day, and its virtue really is in its also having an important effect on the internal situation. The method of its operation on the internal situation is that the higher bank rate would mean curtailment of credit, that the curtailment of credit would diminish enterprise and cause unemployment, and that that unemployment would tend to bring down wages and costs of production generally. . . .

Mr. MONTAGU NORMAN: I should imagine that, as you have stated it, that is the orthodox theory, taking a long view, and as such, I should subscribe to it—I could not dispute it with you.

Thus, Mr. Norman was forced to admit, but only under great pressure, every one of the devastating effects which, according to the Cunliffe Report, followed from the raising of the bank rate; with the added effect of a tendency to bring down wages. The Macmillan Report put the issue beyond all question in the following passages:

For consider how bank rate policy works out in such a case. Its efficacy depends in the first instance on reducing the profits of business men. When, in the effort to minimise this result, output and employment are contracted, it depends upon decreasing the amount of business profits, and increasing unemployment up to whatever figure is necessary to cause business men either to decrease their costs by additional economies or to insist on, and their workers to accept, a reduction of wages. But public opinion does not easily acquiesce in such a process. And the reduction, if and when effected, will fall unequally and unfairly on those sections of the community who are least protected by contract, least able to defend themselves, and often least able to afford the sacrifice.

And:

Moreover, once such a condition of depression has become firmly established, a policy of dear money will no longer be necessary to ensure its continuance; for it will contain within itself the seeds of its own perpetuation.

Thus, it is an unquestioned and admitted fact that the management of a gold standard entails at times a disastrous curtailment of internal industry and trade. The return of Britain to a gold standard in 1925 was effected in such circumstances that this disastrous intervention was not occasional and spasmodic, but permanent and continuous. As the Macmillan Report states:

Great Britain established a gold parity which meant that her existing level of sterling incomes and cash was relatively too high in terms of gold, so that, failing a downward adjustment, those of her industries which are subject to foreign competition, were put at an artificial disadvantage.

The "downward adjustment" here mentioned is a short and euphemistic term for the tragic and appalling list of industrial disasters specified in the Cunliffe Report as being the result of raising the bank rate. The return to a gold standard in 1925 placed Britain between the devil and the deep sea. Either she had to submit to this artificially induced industrial depression or she had to lose her export industries. The gold standard is placing the countries on the gold bloc in the same dilemma to-day.

The term "artificial" in the above extract from the Macmillan Report is eloquent of the fact that there were no natural reasons for the eclipse of Britain's commercial and industrial prosperity between 1925 and 1931. It was an artificially produced and prolonged industrial depression. In the words of Mr. Keynes:

> For at least fifty years before the war—perhaps for more than a hundred years—we had had no experience of a rapid and cold-blooded Income Deflation on anything like this scale. . . . The authorities at the Treasury and at the Bank of England . . . greatly over-estimated the efficacy of their weapons of credit restriction and bank rate when applied, with the object of producing out of the blue a cold-blooded income deflation.

Mr. Hawtrey emphasises the artificial nature of the prolonged industrial depression induced by the return to the gold standard in 1925, by pointing out that it involved "a conspicuous departure from former practice." During the nineteenth century the drastic step of raising the bank rate had been reserved for boom periods of abnormal and feverish activity. The deflation initiated in 1924, leading up to the raising of the bank rate to 5 per cent in March 1925, was not required to cure any such derangement. There was no boom, no crisis, no speculation, no threat to the banks' reserves. It was the first and only occasion in currency history in which the severe brake of deflation had been deliberately applied to the country during a period of recovery from depression. What the country needed in 1924–25 was a gentle stimulant suited to a patient in a forward stage of convalescence after a severe illness. What the Bank of England administered was a dangerous drug usually reserved as a potent sedative to be cautiously administered to a patient in a violent spasm of delirium.

Despite the depression, the unemployment and the wholesale dislocation of internal industry and trade, resulting from a rise in the bank rate, the amazing fiction that the gold standard was automatic in its operation was invented and assiduously promulgated. By concentrating on the initial action of the bank, and on its final objective, the protection of the gold reserves, and by resolutely ignoring the hundred and one disasters to industry comprising the intermediate stages, it was possible to pretend that the movements of gold were governed automatically by the movements of the bank rate. It was a monumental piece of pretence. Instead of being automatic, the gold standard was maintained by the deliberate and calculated subordination of the internal prosperity of the country to the stabilisation of the foreign exchanges.

Mr. Montagu Norman has explained how it was possible for such an obvious fiction to gain credence. In his evidence to the Macmillan Commission on March 26, 1930, he stated:

A year or two ago we were forced, as I think, to look closely at the position of industry in this country, with which previously we had practically no direct contact, and with which, as a Central Bank, many persons think that even now we should have nothing to do.

Thus, although the Bank of England had no direct contact with the position on industry in the country, it had the power to depress enterprise, to slacken the progress of industry, to create unemployment, to bring manufacturers and merchants to ruin, and to cause all the disasters and dislocations to industry described in the Cunliffe Report. Being completely aloof from these reactions to its policy, it was possible to assume that they were not of much consequence, and that it was producing its ultimate results automatically.

The fiction of the automatic operation of the gold standard gained ready credence in banking and financial circles of the City of London. As related in Chapter II, the dominant form of currency now in circulation (variously known under the designations of bank money, cheques and deposits) is created by bankers, and is an encroachment on the sovereignty of Government as the sole authority for the creation and issue of money. The fiction of the automatic action of the gold standard was an excellent weapon to camouflage this encroachment on the province of Government, and to prevent Government from resuming full control of the circulation of this form of money. Any proposals for currency reform, or any suggestions that Government should intervene to protect commerce and industry from the more flagrant evils of artificial currency deflation, were characterised by such epithets as "currency manipulation" and "juggling with the currency."

The Bank of England, in its exalted position of aloofness from the position of industry in the country, could juggle with employment, juggle with wages, juggle with the profits of merchants and manufacturers. But for the Government to intervene to protect trade, employment, wages and profits from the devastating effects of such jugglery was regarded with deep resentment by the banking and financial interests of the City of London.

The Macmillan Report ruthlessly demolished this flimsy pretence, stating:

> The monetary system of this country must be a managed system. It is not advisable, or indeed practicable, to regard our monetary system as an automatic system, grinding out the right results by the operation of natural forces, aided by a few maxims of general application and some well-worn rules of thumb.

And:

> The action to be taken, and the precise moment at which it should be taken, remain in the sphere of discretion and judgment, in a word with "management." That the sphere of "management" in this sense is wide and responsible is beyond doubt.

The fiction of currency automatism was finally and effectually laid to rest by the British Empire Currency Declaration of 1933 (see Appendix II) stating that the restoration of a satisfactory international monetary standard requires—

the deliberate management of the international standard in such a manner as to ensure the smooth and efficient working of international trade and finance.

The gold standard was excellently suited to the conditions of the nineteenth century. Britain's commercial pre-eminence, and her position as the one outstanding creditor nation in the world, enabled her to give it a unity of direction and administration impossible in the post-war world. Her wide international commerce and extensive foreign investments, made her interests coincide with those of the younger nations in an early stage of development, and enabled her to minimise and overcome its many defects. The attempt to resuscitate it after the war had disastrous effects. The United States had already modified it out of all resemblance to the pre-war gold standard. The conflicting conceptions of the methods and objectives of the gold standard ultimately brought both nations to the verge of disaster.

In Chapter III a question by Mr. Cross was quoted, asking whether it would not have a terrific effect on the people of Britain if they knew that there was no chance of going back to the gold standard; and a tentative reply to that question was given. Perhaps a better reply would have been that it would have a terrific effect on the people of Britain if they thought there was the remotest likelihood of a return to the gold standard. The quotation from Mr. Keynes at the head of this chapter is but a faint and watery under-statement of the intense feelings with which the people of Britain regard the gold standard. They attribute to it the national losses and humiliations of the most disastrous period of British history.

An explanation of the hostility of the industrial, commercial, and working classes of Britain to the gold standard is provided by Professor Robbins in an article in *Lloyd's Bank Monthly Review* for October 1932. Mr. Montagu Norman, when giving evidence before the Macmillan Commission, had the grace to be ashamed of the operation of the gold standard from 1925 to 1931 on the internal situation. He endeavoured to minimise its degree of interference with internal industry, and it was only under pressure of a strong cross-examination that he admitted the serious effects of gold standard policy on the internal prosperity of the country.

But Professor Robbins is more royalist than the King. He would intensify the degree of interference of the Bank of England with internal prosperity. He considers that the principal defect of the gold standard policy from 1925 to 1931 was that it was not rigorous enough. He states:

If we are to avoid inflationary disturbances, the authorities in different financial centres must work the gold standard on lines much more severe than those which have been the rule in recent years.

In order that there shall be no doubt as to his conception of what the monetary policy of Britain should be, he expresses it in the terms:

But, above all, policy must be directed to restoring the freedom of the market in the widest sense of the term. By this I mean not only the lowering of tariffs and the abolition of trade restrictions, but also the removal of those causes which produce internal rigidity—rigid wages, rigid prices, rigid systems of production—which in the period since the war, have deprived the economic mechanism, particularly in this country, of its power of adaptation to external change.

Professor Robbins' favourite term of abuse is "rigid." He dislikes the insistence by Trade Unions and Trade Boards that rates of wages must sustain a reasonable standard of living; so he denounces it as the system of "rigid wages." He approves the gold standard policy of forcing merchants and manufacturers to sell their goods at a loss, as described by the Cunliffe Report of 1918; so he denounces the system of "rigid prices." He assumes an ignorance of the fact, stressed in the Macmillan Report, that the return to the gold standard in 1925 was effected at so high a parity that all British industries subject to foreign competition were put at an artificial disadvantage; so he insults British manufacturers by the phrase "rigid systems of production."

But, much as Professor Robbins dislikes rigidity, there is one form of rigidity that moves him to the highest form of admiration, the rigid fixity of the price of gold at £3 17s. 9d. to £3 17s. 10½d. per ounce. That rigidity, which in the words of Dr. Sprague, Financial Adviser to the Bank of England, reduced the British gold reserves "to the last sovereign which there was in the Bank," is the one true rigidity which must be preserved at all costs. Reduced wages, vanished profits, export industries artificially killed, the Bank of England reduced to its last sovereign— all these must be gladly and thankfully endured in order that the sanctity and the rigidity of the gold standard may be preserved, and that Britain may possess the "power of adaptation to external change," that is, the power to adapt itself to the hoarding mentality of the Continent.

Professor Robbins' article exhibits the gold standard mentality in the raw. He gives a doctrinaire defence of an outworn and obsolete system of currency, inspired by a complete misunderstanding of the working of the British industrial system. Published in a banking review, it was an appeal to the banking interests of the City of London to rally at the forthcoming World Economic Conference to defeat the new system of international currency recently inaugurated at Ottawa. It provides unconsciously, in a concentrated form, the reasons why the mercantile, industrial and labour classes of the country distrust the gold standard so intensely, and why Britain will never go back to gold. It explains the testimony given by General Wood, President of Sears, Roebuck & Co., of Chicago, to the effect that :

The manufacturers and merchants of Northern England are as bitterly opposed to the monetary policies of Mr. Montagu Norman in charge of the Bank of England as our manufacturers in this country were opposed to going off gold. The hardest words I heard about Mr. Montagu Norman were in England, and not in this country. They said he had crucified the manufacturers and merchants of England when he changed the pound in England, as was done.

In Chapter II eight popular criticisms of the banking system were presented. Much of the explanation and the justification for these criticisms will be found in this chapter. The disastrous effects of the operation of raising the bank rate on commerce and industry in order to maintain the gold standard, as cynically revealed by the Cunliffe Report; the attempt of Mr. Montagu Norman to minimise the harm caused by that operation; the revealing clarity of the Macmillan Report of the inequitable and unfair results on those members of the community "least able to defend themselves"; the artificial placing of British export industries at a disadvantage; the cold-blooded income deflation of 1924–25; the incompetent diagnosis which administered a potent currency sedative to a patient urgently in need of a moderate stimulant; the impudent fiction that the gold standard was automatic in its operation; the complacent admission that the Bank of England had previously "practically no direct contact" with the position of industry in this country; and, perhaps above all, Professor Robbins' arrogant assumption that wages, prices and systems of production should be completely subject to the bankers and the banking system, which should work the gold standard on lines much more severe than those that had been the rule in recent years; these explain, and to a great extent justify, the criticisms levied against the banking system, and the demand that it should be brought much more in contact with commerce and industry by a measure of increased Government control.

CHAPTER V

THE AMERICAN CURRENCY
REVOLUTION, 1922

Mr. WILLIAMSON: "Do you think that the Federal Reserve Board could, as a matter of fact, stabilise price levels to a greater extent than they have in the past, by giving greater expansion to market operations and restriction or extension of credit facilities?"

Governor STRONG: "I, personally, think that the administration of the Federal Reserve System, since the reaction in 1921, has been just as nearly directed as reasonable human wisdom could direct it, toward that very object."—United States Congress Committee on Stabilisation.

THE above question and answer express, in a brief compass, the nature of the Currency Revolution effected by the United States in 1922. They make it clear that the Federal Reserve Board had transformed the gold standard from a currency system, whose main objective was the stability of the international exchanges, into a system devoted primarily to the stability of prices. The Revolution had been foreshadowed at the Genoa Currency Conference held early in 1922. That Conference sought a remedy for the principal defect of the pre-war gold standard. Prior to the war, the gold standard had stabilised the price of gold, that is, its value expressed in terms of currency; but it had not stabilised the purchasing power of gold, that is, its value expressed in goods. Though the price had remained stable at £3 17s. 10½d.

per ounce for ninety-two years, its purchasing power over goods had varied considerably.

The members of the Genoa Conference were apprehensive that future variations in the purchasing power of gold would probably be much greater than in the past. The power of Britain to exercise unitary control of the operation of a gold standard had vanished. If a number of nations were to come on to the gold standard in the near future, the demand for gold to provide them with adequate reserves would lead to a competitive scramble which would upset both the price and the purchasing power of gold. The Conference therefore recommended Central Banks to co-ordinate the demand for gold to avoid the wide fluctuations of purchasing power, which might otherwise result from the simultaneous and competitive efforts of a number of countries to secure metallic reserves.

This was a revolutionary idea. The gold standard had hitherto been concerned with the stabilisation of the international exchanges. The Genoa Conference recommended that it should be equally concerned with the stabilisation of prices or of purchasing power. It was to perform what had hitherto been regarded not only as being beyond the scope of the currency authorities, but also as being quite impossible of achievement. It was to reconcile stability of prices with stability of the international exchanges.

Hawtrey expresses the nature of the change implied in the following passages:

The Genoa Resolutions of 1922 mark an epoch in the evolution of the art (of Central Banking) in that, for the first time, they establish the responsibility of the central banks for the value of gold.

And:

The gold standard would be maintained, but gold would be tied to the currency units, instead of the currency units to gold.

The gold standard, in short, was to be turned inside out. Its defects were to be remedied by transforming it into a standard of quite another nature. The fluctuations in the purchasing powers of gold, which the Genoa Conference sought to prevent, could have been determined only with reference to a Price Index. Stability of purchasing power would inevitably mean a Price Index standard of value. Gold would no longer be the standard of value. Its value would be controlled by the movements of the price level on a Price Index. The value of gold would be a purely token value, determined by the co-operation of the central banks in accordance with the movements of the price level, and not by the operation of the law of supply and demand in a free and competitive market.

The recommendations of the Genoa Conference, like the recommendations of the Macmillan Report, would have abolished the gold standard in fact, while retaining its appearance to disguise the nature of the change to be effected. Gold was to be retained because of its prestige, because of its age-long tradi-

74

tion, because of the metallic complex of most of the peoples of the world. But the real currency standard was to be the world wholesale Price Index. Gold was to supply the glitter, the glamour, the resplendent frontage, but the real work would be effected behind the scenes by regulating the value of gold in accordance with the tendency of the price level to depart from equilibrium as measured in a Price Index.

The main Genoa recommendations were never adopted. Its valuable, but subsidiary, proposals that Gold Exchange Standard methods should be followed by the nations returning to the gold standard were accepted, and eased the strain considerably as nation after nation returned to gold. To the extent that reserves were held in foreign exchange instead of in gold, a great economy in the use of gold was effected. But the relief was temporary. The Gold Exchange Standard gradually lost its popularity. Its methods were subsequently revived unexpectedly by the creation of the British Exchange Equalisation Fund. (See Chapter X and Appendix IV).

The main recommendation of the Genoa Conference, that the central banks should co-operate to control the purchasing power of gold, was never adopted. But though never adopted by the central banks as a whole, it was adopted as an internal policy by the Federal Reserve Board of the United States under the leadership of General Strong. The economists of the United States have always shown a great interest in the stabilisation of prices or purchasing power ever since Professor Irving Fisher made his famous proposal for a compensated dollar. As developed, his proposals were, on a limited national scale, substantially the same as the main recommendations of the Genoa Conference.

The United States has no central institution like the Bank of England for the control of currency. There are twelve regional Reserve Banks situated at the twelve most important financial centres of the country. They are responsible, under the control of the Federal Reserve Board, comprising one representative from each bank, for the issue of the currency and credit required to finance and maintain the agriculture, industry and trade of the country. The Federal Reserve System was established in 1913 for the purpose of controlling currency in much the same manner as that function is performed by the Bank of England.

But, in actual practice, the working of the Federal Reserve System departed widely from that of the Bank of England. In place of singleness of aim and unity of control, there was diversity of purpose and disunity of action. Mr. Frank A. Vanderlip, an eminent American banker, who assisted in the drafting of the Federal Reserve Act, has given the following explanation of its actual working:

In the Federal Reserve there are thirteen entities at the wheel, the twelve Federal Reserve Governors, and their organisations, and a Central Authority here in Washington, that is not altogether an authority. We find Federal Reserve Banks at the same moment, with one policy in regard to rates, and another with the opposite policy. We have seen open-market operations carried on in exactly opposite ways by two Federal Reserve Banks at the same time. They are not co-ordinated into a unified force.

After the war this unwieldly and amorphous system was reduced to unity and order by the genius and personality of Governor Strong. He formed an Open Market Committee, comprising the Governors of the four strongest Reserve Banks, to control and co-ordinate the purchase and sale of securities on behalf of the Board. He concentrated in the New York Reserve Bank most of the short-term operations, and as much as he possibly could of the re-discounting operations of the Board. Under his direction the Federal Reserve Board attained a unity of policy and an efficiency of control never before achieved.

This reform was effected just in time to save the United States from a serious financial crisis. The post-war inflation in Britain and the United States culminated in 1920, and was met by the application of similar policies of severe deflation of currency and credit in both countries. The resulting depression of trade, exactly according to plan, as specified in the Cunliffe Report, went much farther than was intended, and was remedied by a moderate relaxation of credit and an expansion of currency in 1922.

This caused a steady progress towards prosperity in both Britain and the United States. Although Britain was off the gold standard at the time, and the United States was on a gold standard, their currency policies were carefully co-ordinated with each other.

77

But at this point the United States was faced with the same problem which had confronted Britain in the early days of the gold standard. A strong creditor position, with a high protectionist policy, resulted in the steady movement of gold to the United States. Britain had solved the problem in the previous century by adopting Free Trade. The United States was not prepared to adopt such a solution.

Nevertheless some solution was imperative. Gold was coming into the United States at the rate of 400 million dollars per annum. According to the pre-war conception of the gold standard, this should have resulted in a cheap money policy and a general raising of prices. According to the Macmillan Report:

> Countries which are receiving gold must be prepared to act on a policy which will have the effect of raising prices.

Also:

> The nineteenth-century philosophy of the gold standard was based on the assumption that an increase of gold in the vaults of the Central Banks would imply a "cheap" money policy, and that a cheap money policy would affect the entire price structure and the level of money incomes in the country concerned.

Now the maximum amount of all kinds of currency (gold, notes and bank money) in the United States is governed by two proportions. The note issue is limited to two and a half times the gold reserve. Bank money is governed by an elaborate series of proportions, but the general resultant is that bank money is about ten times the amount of the reserves of the commercial banks with the Federal Reserve Banks. The ten to one proportion is a universally accepted assumption, but the following authorities may be cited:

The Annual Report of the Federal Reserve Board for 1924 states:

> The ratio between reserve balances maintained by member banks at the reserve banks, to member banks deposit liabilities has remained practically constant at 10 per cent, which represents on the average the minimum required by law.

The Macmillan Report states:

> In the United States . . . the proportion of reserves to deposits actually held has in practice worked out in recent years at a percentage between 7 and 9 per cent of deposits in addition to till money of about 2 per cent, making in practice about 9·5 per cent altogether.

Thus the total circulation of currency in the United States is governed by the two proportions:

i. Notes may be $2\frac{1}{2}$ times the gold reserves.
ii. Bank money is about ten times the amount of the reserves of the commercial banks with the Reserve Banks.

It is not possible to work out an exact proportion of total currency (gold, notes and bank money) to the gold reserves, because of the amount of gold and notes in actual circulation. But it is usually assumed that it is possible to expand the total currency in circulation to a volume of ten to twelve times the gold reserves.

Assuming the lower proportion, ten to one, the annual inflow of gold into the United States, amounting on an average to 400 million dollars, would have meant, under traditional gold standard principles, an annual increase of currency of 4,000 million dollars. This would have produced inflation on an enormous scale. It was a contingency which the traditional gold standard had never contemplated, and which could not be met by normal gold standard methods. Governor Strong and the Federal Reserve Board were faced with this dilemma: Should they adhere to the traditional gold standard, and subject the United States to wild and almost boundless inflation? Or should they protect the United States from inflation by departing from the traditional gold standard?

Hawtrey describes their decision in the following terms:

At this critical juncture, the authorities in control of the Federal Reserve System deliberately departed from that mechanical subservience to reserve proportions which had previously been supposed essential to the art of central banking.

In other words, they effected a Currency Revolution. They modified the gold standard into something fundamentally different from what it had hitherto been. The United States remained on a gold standard, but not on the gold standard of tradition. The gold standard of tradition would have produced a degree of currency expansion resulting in excessive inflation. The revolutionary currency system inaugurated by the Federal Reserve Board in 1922 was adopted with the distinct objective of protecting the United States from an orgy of inflation, which would have been induced by adherence to the traditional gold standard.

It cannot be too strongly insisted that in the United States in the year 1922 the traditional gold standard policy was a strongly inflative force, and that it was the Federal Reserve Board's policy of sterilisation of gold which was fighting the inflation of the traditional gold standard. An opinion has gathered currency that Governor Strong's policy was the cause of the inflation which resulted in the disasters of 1929 and 1933. The exact contrary is the case. The Macmillan Report recognises that his policy was a decided anti-inflation policy in the passage:

> Broadly speaking, the United States continued throughout the post-war period to gain gold, until by the middle of May 1927 the gold stock of the U.S.A. reached the maximum figure of 4,700 million dollars. It had been the avowed policy of the Federal Reserve authorities to regard this stock as a trust fund, and therefore to prevent such an expansion of credit in the United States as would necessitate the permanent retention of the whole stock as a permanent reserve. The policy of gold sterilisation was the objective expression of this point of view.

The traditional gold standard policy having been abandoned, it was necessary to decide what was to be the main objective of the new transformed standard. This objective was supplied by the recommendations of the Genoa Conference. Although the Central Banks of the world had refused to co-operate to stabilise the purchasing price of gold, it was quite feasible for the Federal Reserve Board to stabilise the purchasing price of the dollar. That was the objective of the new Federal Reserve policy.

It was operated by sterilising a certain amount of the gold received by the Federal Reserve Banks. A very close watch was kept on the Wholesale Price Index, an elaborate weighted average of the wholesale prices of commodities in use in the United States. If the price level tended to go up, it was an indication that there was too much currency in circulation, and restrictive measures were adopted. If the price level tended to go down, it was an indication that there was too little currency in circulation and credit was relaxed. Instead of credit and bank money being based on the total gold reserves, only sufficient gold was allowed to function to keep the dollar at a stable level. The rest was sterilised.

This policy was the personal policy of Governor Strong, adopted by the Federal Reserve Board under the inspiration of his genius and the strength of his personality. The policy of stabilising the dollar was neither prescribed by law, nor dictated by Government, nor evolved by the collective wisdom of the members of the Federal Reserve Board. Although strongly supported by the full weight of the Agricultural and Farm Organisations of the country, the Currency Revolution effected in 1922 was officially and financially a one-man revolution. Mr. F. A. Vanderlip has testified to the following effect:

Remember that their (the Federal Reserve System) purpose is to offer a means of a unified reserve system, a reservoir of reserves, and to loan to member banks. Their purpose has never been, by law, or even by action, to hold the price level without fluctuation.

Yet the evidence of Governor Strong, as quoted at the head of this chapter, demonstrates that the policy of stabilising the price level had been pursued by the Federal Reserve Board as nearly as reasonable human wisdom could direct it, since the reaction in 1921. It was a great personal triumph to have persuaded the Federal Reserve System to adopt a policy that its constitution did not contemplate, to have effected a revolution in the operation of a gold standard with a century of success behind it, to have stabilised the dollar, and to have evolved a currency system which carried the United States to the highest pitch of prosperity in its history.

The 1922 Currency Revolution in the United States should not be compared with that effected by Britain in 1816. Rather should it be compared with the momentous currency discoveries of Sir Isaac Newton, made a century previously, from 1700 to 1717. By practical experiment Newton discovered the Quantity Theory of Money, and paved the way for such memorable currency events as the stabilisation of the guinea and the establishment of the gold standard. So Governor Strong, by practical experiment, discovered the way to the elusive equilibrium position which separated Inflation from Deflation. He invented Reflation. He made Reflation a practical policy, and a successful policy. It was a tragedy that illness caused him to relinquish control of the Federal Reserve Board shortly before his death in 1928, just as his policy was about to undergo its most crucial test.

The fiscal policy of the United States accentuated the divergence between the new dollar stabilisation standard and the traditional gold standard. For convenience they may be referred to under the designations "the sterling standard" and "the dollar standard" respectively. The sterling standard had been associated with Free Trade. The dollar standard was associated with Protection. A mere catalogue of their divergencies would be lengthy. The sterling standard was international; the dollar standard national. The sterling standard stabilised the international exchanges; the dollar standard the national price level. The sterling standard settled the international Balance of Trade by goods; the dollar standard with gold. The sterling standard economised gold; the dollar standard sterilised gold. The sterling standard protected the debtor countries from gold depletion; the dollar standard drained them of gold. The sterling standard fostered the development of backward countries; the dollar standard fostered internal development. The sterling standard stimulated the trade cycle; the dollar standard restrained it.

And so the list might proceed, but sufficient divergencies have been mentioned to demonstrate that though the sterling standard and the dollar standard were both gold standards, they had little else in common. The phrase "on the gold standard" has no meaning. There are, and have been, so many possible gold standards, that without some definite description of the nature of the gold standard, to which reference is being made, no clear statement is possible. The term "the gold standard" means anything or nothing, usually the latter.

It meant disaster when Britain returned to a gold standard in 1925. From 1922 to 1924, although the United States was on a gold standard and Britain was not, the currency policies of the two countries proceeded in perfect harmony. Both proceeded together in a gradual progress towards prosperity. But when in 1925 Britain returned to a gold standard, conflict became inevitable. Though both countries were on gold standards, their previous harmonious currency policies became discordant. The consideration of their conflict must be reserved for a subsequent chapter. For the present it is sufficient to draw attention to the fact that the bitterness and intensity of the conflict is evidence of the fundamental difference between the two gold standards effected by the Currency Revolution of 1922.

The prosperity of the United States continued as long as its destinies were under the control of the genius of Governor Strong. But there was one vital weakness in his policy. It was purely personal. It was not sanctioned by law, nor had it attained the prestige of a lengthy operation. The moment his guiding hand was withdrawn, his dollar stabilisation policy was abandoned. He left no successor capable of continuing his work or of shouldering his responsibilities. The Federal Reserve Board reverted to a state of chaos and internal dissension. With Governor Strong's death, the United States reverted to a vacillating policy based on a confused appreciation of the methods of operating the traditional gold standard. The country abandoned the protection against inflation which Governor Strong had laboured so hard to construct, and so patiently to maintain, and proceeded rapidly towards inflation and disaster.

But Governor Strong's labours were not lost. His currency policy formed the basis of the similar but broader and more comprehensive international policy which was to be inaugurated by Britain at Ottawa in 1932, ten years after his own experiment had been initiated. The Ottawa Policy has been endorsed by President Roosevelt in his message to the World Economic Conference on July 3, 1933. It is quite possible that Governor Strong's Currency Revolution, effected in 1922, will eventually result in a joint Anglo-American system of international currency that will lead the world back to prosperity, and wipe out the uphappy memories of the tragic decline and fall of the gold standard.

CHAPTER VI

THE CURRENCY CONFLICT

"The United States, ever since 1924, had been opposing the British policy of credit restriction with measures of credit relaxation. In the summer of 1927 the credit relaxation was intensified. That may be regarded as the response of the American attempt in stabilisation to the new complication of an international gold standard."—Mr. R. C. HAWTREY.

THE American Currency Revolution of 1922, establishing a policy of dollar stabilisation, did not prejudice the harmonious relations between British and American currency policies which had continued since the war. The internal policy of dollar stabilisation suited conditions in the United States admirably. The British currency policy, by which the pound sterling was allowed to find its natural level, was equally admirably suited to British conditions, both internally and externally. The two countries were proceeding harmoniously together on policies which, though not identical, did not clash with each other. For both countries the worst financial disturbances of the war were over, less than three years after the war had terminated.

There were, of course, many unsettled war problems, war debts, reparations, and the heavy currency inflations on the continent of Europe. But the two principal countries of the world had found their way back to prosperity. Production was leaping upwards with unprecedented rapidity. The destruction of wealth during the war was being repaired more rapidly than anyone had considered possible. Britain's return to prosperity was as pronounced as that of the United States. Unemployment, in two years, dropped from 2,000,000 to less than 1,000,000. If only prosperity could have continued for some years longer at this pace, all the outstanding problems of the war could have been settled with ease.

It is worth while examining the currency policy of Britain during these two years of remarkable recovery, 1922–24. It can be studied in the evidence of Dr. Sprague, contained in Appendix IV to this volume. It is true that Dr. Sprague's evidence relates to the British currency policy of 1931–34. But that policy was simply a reversion to the earlier policy of 1922–24, supplemented by the assistance of the Exchange Equalisation Fund. Dr. Sprague is concerned with repudiating the American insinuations that Britain was using the Exchange Equalisation Fund to depreciate the value of the pound with reference to the dollar, in order to give the British exports an advantage over American exports. He repeats his repudiation again and again, as will be seen from the following passages:

From that time [September 1931] to this [February 1934] it has been the policy of the British Government to exert no influence calculated to depreciate the pound, but to endeavour to strengthen it and to smooth off the fluctuations.

It became clear that the British Government was not disposed to do anything to weaken the pound.

The objective of British policy in this matter is comparatively narrow. If they had attempted to fix the price of sterling at some figure relative to the dollar and the franc, which would have been impossible, they would have required an immense fund. However, that has not been the objective in view at any time.

They have taken what they call a neutral policy with regard to the value of the pound.

It has operated so that influential financial circles have felt that the pound can be made reasonably stable.

Through a certain process of trial and error, an equilibrium may be reached, so that the value would be determined.

That policy of allowing the pound to find its neutral, or natural, value was the British currency policy both in 1922–24 and in 1931–34. The neutral, or natural, value of the pound is determined by world price parity, the operation of which is akin to, but not identical with, Professor Gustav Cassell's well-known theory of purchasing power parity. It is based on the fact that sea communication is so cheap and so efficient that there is now one single world wholesale price level throughout the world for each primary commodity in general demand, while it is on the high seas. For, should any price variation arise at any port, cargoes would at once be deflected from the port of consignment to the port where the highest price would be obtainable. The theory is only true for cargoes in transit, because once they are landed they become subject to the operation of tariffs. A slight modification of the theory is necessary to allow for the different costs of transport to different ports, but this is trifling in comparison with the value of the cargo.

While off the gold standard, Britain must adjust its costs of production to this uniform world price level. If the pound is at too high a value in the foreign exchange market, British costs will be too high to compete in the world market. British exports will, accordingly, fall. The fall of British exports means that foreign importers will not want so much sterling to pay for them. The reduced demand for sterling brings its value down in the foreign exchange market until it is at its natural, or neutral, level.

Similarly, if the pound is at too low a level, British costs will be low, British exports will expand, the demand for the sterling to pay for them will increase, and the value of the pound will rise in the foreign exchange market till it reaches its natural level.

It was under this policy of allowing the pound to find its natural level that Britain made such a remarkable recovery from 1922 to 1924. That policy suited Britain exactly as the dollar stabilisation policy suited America. There is every reason to believe that, if this policy had been continued, British prosperity would have kept pace with that of the United States.

But the promise of returning prosperity induced the Bank of England to conceive the mad idea of returning to the pre-war gold standard. For once Britain's instinct and capacity for currency administration failed her. This fatal move was the result of a series of errors, blunders, miscalculations, and blindnesses that are now inconceivable. So numerous are they that it is much easier to present them in the form of a catalogue than by means of a narrative. The following list gives, in a condensed form, the factors that were not seen, not appreciated, and not allowed for, when the return to a gold standard was under consideration:

    i. Pre-war conditions had vanished never to return.

    ii. In particular, Britain had lost her commercial pre-eminence, and her unique position as the sole outstanding creditor nation, which gave unity to the pre-war gold standard.

    iii. For the future, Britain must share the management and control of the gold standard with the United States and with France, two countries with fiscal and currency practices and mentalities widely different from those of Britain.

    iv. The rules of the gold standard administration (the rules of the game) had in the past been formulated and enforced by Britain. There was no reason to believe that the United States and France would observe them.

    v. The United States had made a complete revolution in the methods and objectives of the gold standard, and was administering it on principles quite foreign to the pre-war gold standard.

    vi. The metallic psychologies of the United States and of France differed widely from each other and from that of Britain, and would be certain to introduce disharmonies in the operation of a metallic standard.

    vii. The protectionist policies of the United States and France would result in a drain of gold to these countries, which would deflate the currencies of the rest of the world.

    viii. The London Money Market would be completely disorganised by the continuous drain of gold from the debtor nations to the United States and France.

    ix. The return of Britain towards prosperity was due to

the fact that the pound sterling was free to find its natural value in the foreign exchange market.

x. The return to gold would involve a forcible dislocation of the pound sterling from its natural value to a position 10 per cent above its natural value.

xi. The artificially high value of the pound would involve severe and continuous deflation, with all the disastrous consequences to internal industry and trade described in the Cunliffe Report.

xii. France and Italy had greatly depreciated currencies, and if, as was probable, they returned to gold at a depreciated value, the handicap to Britain of an artificially high value of the pound would be intensified.

xiii. The revived practice of hoarding on the continent of Europe, added to the inevitable accumulations of gold by the protectionist countries, would seriously curtail the amount of gold available for currency, and add to the severity of the deflation resulting from the return to gold.

xiv. Above all, the administration of two different gold standards by Britain and the United States would lead inevitably to a currency conflict between the two countries.

These are not wisdom-after-the-event inferences and deductions. They are facts and reactions which were as ascertainable in 1924 and 1925 as they are to-day. But the aloofness of the Bank of England from the industrial and commercial interests of the country, admitted by Mr. Montagu Norman, and its preoccupation with the problems of international finance, made it an easy victim to the desire for a return to "the good old times." The Bank of England acted as if under the illusion that by a process of currency manipulation it could transform the world back into the nineteenth century. The world must be made to conform to the nineteenth-century conception of currency rather than that an obsolete system of currency should be brought up-to-date to suit modern post-war conditions.

The Bank of England had ample warning of the disaster that the course it contemplated would bring to British industry. The Federation of British Industries made a gallant attempt to get behind the veil of aloofness with which the Bank of England was shrouded from all contact with, or knowledge of, industrial England. It protested in weighty and dignified language, which proved ultimately to be prophetic, against the artificial infliction of incalculable disasters to industry in the interests of an outworn system of currency. But, unfortunately, its protests were made to a committee under the chairmanship of Lord Bradbury, a Treasury official with a nineteenth-century mentality. They were regarded as the amateur instrusions of a body of outsiders into the sacred mysteries of currency and finance, and were calmly ignored.

The attitude of the labour world is best presented in the language of Mr. Bevin, a member of the Macmillan Commission. He had listened with patience to the cynical evidence of Mr. Montagu Norman with his preoccupation with international finance, and his attitude of aloofness and patronage towards industry; and finally addressed him in these terms:

You are a Governor of the Bank of England. I am a Trade Union Official. That is the point we have to face across the table. I am taking from 1921 up to the panel of 1924; I am meeting the industrialists who do not know anything that is in the mind of the Bank of England on the financial policy of the country. They have no knowledge that you are going to interfere, that you are going to restore the gold standard, that you are going to do anything. We met morally the first period of deflation in 1921 when the first step to deflation was taken. We knew that we had to face a heavy reduction in money wages to get a post-war adjustment. We proceeded from 1921 onwards meeting employers across the table and getting that post-war adjustment to a new price. Contracts have been fixed on that new price, new standards have been marked out, men are becoming adjusted to that level of earnings, to everything on the new basis. Suddenly the whole thing is upset by the steps taken in 1925, which throws every bit of work, which the two parties in industry have done, out of gear. We are faced with rising unemployment, bitter disputes, and a new level of wages to be fixed, without notice, without consideration, without guide, without any indication what its object is. I ask you, Mr. Norman, if industry is placed in a position like that, whether or not you do not think the misfortune of the jam is inevitable?

What a living picture that gives of the world of industry as it is; employers and employed, actively engaged in adjusting industry to post-war conditions; heavy reductions of wages accepted by the Trade Unions on behalf of the men; new prices adjusted; contracts fixed on the new prices and the new level of earnings. What a contrast it affords to the world of fantasy conjured out of Professor Robbins' imagination: "rigid wages, rigid prices, rigid systems of production."

The above statement of Mr. Bevin explains, in living

and picturesque language, the disastrous nature of the intervention of the Bank of England on the return to prosperity, which was proceeding so satisfactorily up to the middle of 1924. It is a picture of the "automatic" working of the process described in more stately language in the Cunliffe Committee Report. Professor Robertson summarises the effect of the dislocation on this recovery of prosperity in the sentence:

It was clear that between October 1924 and May 1925 the British export trades found an increasing weight upon their shoulders as compared with the previous eighteen months, and that, by the decisive act of May, that weight was riveted round their necks.

The picturesque nature of the phrases used to describe the gold standard, and the action of the Bank of England in forcing it upon Britain in 1925, are sufficient to explain why Britain will never go back to the gold standard. They include: under the harrow (Mr. Montagu Norman); weight riveted round their necks (Robertson); the new complication (Hawtrey); disastrous inefficiency, economic losses, and cold-blooded income deflation (Keynes); drastic deflation, dislocation of trade, increase in unemployment, severe check to export trade (Federation of British Industries); and, misfortune of the jam (Bevin).

The severe dislocation to the internal industry of the country, just as it was settling down to post-war conditions, was supplemented by a prolonged and damaging currency conflict between Britain and the

United States. The Macmillan Report strongly emphasises the necessity for countries on a gold standard to keep carefully in step with each other. But the Macmillan Report did not explain how two countries on two distinct and dissimilar gold standards can keep in step. The confusion is perhaps best illustrated by the following representative opinions as to the nature of the two standards:

Professor Robertson (British):

A truer impression of the state of the world's monetary affairs would be given by saying that America is on an arbitrary standard, while the rest of the world has climbed back, painfully, on to a dollar standard.

Professor Harr (Pennsylvania, United States):

But the European countries were on a gold standard primarily because of the generosity of the United States. They were not on a sound gold standard. The least ripple caused enough confusion to force them off that unsound gold standard.

Sir Robert Kindersley (British):

Although New York professed to be on the gold standard, she never really allowed the gold standard to work properly. . . . America went on her bended knees, almost, to the rest of the world, to adopt the gold standard—but no sooner had she got them to adopt it than she refused to allow it to work.

Mr. Cross (Representative for Texas, United States):

She [Britain] never was really on the gold standard between 1925 and 1931.

Mr. Rand (President, Remington–Rand, United States):

Nor was the United States, really, according to my interpretation, on the gold standard. The gold standard has been fictitious ever since the war, and particularly in this country, since the creation of the Federal Reserve System, when we have been on a managed currency basis, and the world has been, for the most part, on a managed currency basis.

These divergent opinions suggest that the term—the gold standard—has lost all definite meaning. The complete incompatibility between the sterling and the dollar standards after 1925 took the form of different policies of credit and currency control. The United States pursued a policy of reflation with the object of stabilising the dollar price level. Britain had, necessarily, to pursue a policy of deflation, owing to the high level of the pound at which the return to a gold standard was effected. The contradictory policies mutually hampered and obstructed each other.

Britain, naturally, was the worst sufferer; the internal dislocation produced by deflation was accentuated by the international deflation caused by the accumulation and sterilisation of gold in the United States. With the continuous drain of gold, first to the United States only, and subsequently to both the United States and to France, the overseas customers of Britain lost their capacity to buy British goods, and flooded the British market with their products in a desperate attempt to obtain the gold, with which to settle their accounts with France and the United States. The very dominance of the London Money Market was a handicap, spreading depression throughout the world, and placing on London the responsibility for extracting gold from the debtor nations for transmission to France and the United States.

But the United States also felt the effects of the conflict. The fall of world prices, due to the spread of the deflative effects of the British policy, exercised a steady and downward pull on the stabilised dollar. This downward pull was felt particularly on the prices of wheat, cotton, and pork and beef products, which were governed much more by world price levels than by the purchasing price of the dollar. The benefits of a stable dollar were largely neutralised when the prices of agricultural produce were kept at an unduly low level by international influences.

Thus, though the United States had an unprecedented burst of prosperity from 1922 to 1928, the external deflation prevented it from being shared to the full by the agricultural interests of the country. The conflict continued on the lines described in the quotation from Mr. Hawtrey, selected for the heading of this chapter. Reflation in the United States contended with Deflation in the rest of the world. In the year 1928 the confusion was intensified by two events, which in the critical stage towards which the world was drifting amounted to financial disasters. Governor Strong had been prevented for some time by illness from participating in the active work of the Federal

Reserve Board, and passed away in the autumn of 1928. His death caused the Federal Reserve Board to lose the direction, the unity and the promptitude which had been the outstanding qualities of his administration.

The second financial disaster of the year 1928 was the reversion of France from a gold exchange standard to a gold standard of a particularly inflexible and deflatory type. While France was on a gold exchange standard she assisted the reflative efforts of the United States and resisted Britain's deflative policy. But when she transformed her large reserves of foreign exchange into gold, and began to accumulate gold in immense quantities, she accelerated and intensified the deflation due to the policy of Britain.

During the year 1928 there were three conflicting gold standards in operation—in Britain, in the United States and in France. This shattering truth is so clothed in diplomatic language in the following passage from the Macmillan Report that its truth is obscured:

So great in the past ten years have been the reactions of disturbances in one country on conditions on one other that if we were to take the period as a fair criterion, it would be necessary to conclude that the power of the Central Banks, by their joint and several efforts to secure stability, carried a very little way. The Federal Reserve System of the United States has endeavoured to keep that country on an even keel since the war, and yet, even if we ignore the violent movements of the immediate post-war periods, it has been unable to prevent one of the greatest oscillations of boom and collapse in history. Again, the Bank of England has aimed for some years to bring about an equilibrium between this country's conditions and world conditions, but while prices have fallen, costs have remained rigid and the desired equilibrium has not been attained. The Bank of France, restricted by legal enactments, was unable to prevent its vaults being filled with many millions of gold which it did not want.

That passage defines three distinct currency standards, but makes the misleading suggestion that they were operated by "joint and several efforts to secure stability." Instead of being joint and several efforts to secure stability, they were conflicting efforts to realise conflicting conceptions of stability. The endeavour of the United States "to keep that country on an even keel" was the objective of the dollar standard, operated to secure the internal stability of the purchasing power of the dollar. The aim of the Bank of England "to bring about an equilibrium between this country's conditions and the world conditions" was the objective of the sterling standard, operated to secure the external stability of the international exchanges. The filling of the vaults of the Bank of France "with many millions of gold which it did not want" was the resultant (if not the objective) of the hoarding standard, operated to satisfy the French metallic psychology, which insists on using money as a store of savings as well as a medium of exchange.

Thus, during 1928, there were three gold standards in operation, each managed to secure a distinctive objective. At this juncture the Federal Reserve Board found itself without the guiding hand of

Governor Strong. It was alarmed at the rapid growth of speculation, the result of the bounding prosperity of the United States, and of the uneven operation of the dollar stabilisation policy on the agricultural and industrial interests of the country. After months of hesitation and vacillation it dropped the policy of stabilising the dollar, and commenced a policy of deflation with the object of stopping the wave of speculation sweeping through the country. It did not stop speculation, but it succeeded very effectually in stopping the prosperity of the country.

The three gold standards had now one point in common—deflation. At last the three leading commercial nations of the world were in step. But they were in step in the wrong direction. They had their backs to prosperity. They were heading towards bankruptcy and disaster. To Britain, exhausted by a depression which had already lasted over four years, the effect of the triple deflation policies of the three countries was overwhelming. To France, enjoying the artificial prosperity caused by the repudiating devaluation of the franc, deflation brought a progressive decline which has now erased all traces of that short-lived prosperity. To the United States the deflation brought a speedy cessation of the prosperity she had achieved, and a prolonged period of depression and collapse from which she is but now slowly and painfully emerging. To the rest of the world this severe phase of deflation brought deeper depths of stagnation, bankruptcy, and default than had hitherto been attained.

The speculative fever which raged in the United
States in 1928–29 was paralleled by a hoarding fever
which raged on the continent of Europe. It is a mistake
to regard post-war continental hoarding as the patient
laborious addition of franc to franc. It is as feverishly
hectic as any Stock Exchange speculation. Deflation
of currency means the appreciation of gold. The rise
in the sterling price of gold from £3 17s. 10½d. per
ounce to £7 per ounce is as alluring a bait for the
continental hoarder as a similar rise in the price
of a share is to the speculator on the Stock Exchange.
What does it matter to him if he loses the interest on
his non-invested money? That is a trifle. He is grati-
fying his passionate lust for gold, and at the same time
holding an appreciating asset. Hoarding, like speculation, feeds on itself. The insatiable demand for gold
sends up its price, and the increase in its price raises
the profits to be gained by hoarding.

Just as the Federal Reserve Board was forced off
the dollar stabilisation policy by speculation, so the
Bank of England was forced off the gold standard
by speculative hoarding. For ninety-two years, from
1822 to 1914, the Bank of England had successfully
withstood every attack on the sterling price of gold,
£3 17s. 10½d. per ounce. But from 1925 to 1931 it
was faced with a new and unexpected weapon of
attack. The speculative hoarding of gold had no
respect for the fixed price or the fixed purchasing
power of gold. It was an independent force, completely immune from the operation of any of the rules

of currency management. The profits on the use of gold as a speculative counter were greater than the profits to be gained by its use as currency. Naturally, gold forsook the less profitable function, currency, and departed to the more profitable function, hoarding.

The traditional methods of defence only served to stimulate the vigour of the attack. To use two of the picturesque metaphors which have been applied, the deflation policy of the Bank of England placed British industry "under the harrow" and "riveted an increasing weight round the necks" of British exporters. But it could not save the Bank's gold reserves. The higher the bank rate, the stronger the forces tending to appreciate the price of gold. The more the Bank of England used its unique monetary power to collect gold from the uttermost parts of the earth, the more conveniently placed it was to supply the hoarding demand from the Continent.

Gold was the one commodity in the world tending to appreciate in price. And the Bank of England was compelled by law to sell it at a fixed price. Never was there such a golden opportunity for the exchange speculator. It was not speculation; it was a certainty. Gold could be bought at the Bank of England for £3 17s. 10½d. per ounce, and sold at a certain profit to hoarders on the Continent at a higher figure.

This was a post-war contingency with which the gold standard found itself impossible to cope. The Bank of England could control the price of gold if used for currency. It could not control the price of gold if used for hoarding on an extensive scale. The gold standard had completely failed to meet this financial emergency of the post-war world. The situation rapidly became impossible. When the Credit Anstadt failed in May 1931, the flow of gold for continental hoarding grew from a river to a torrent. When the crisis spread to Germany, the torrent increased to an uncontrollable flood. The Bank of England lost £30 millions of gold in July 1931, over £50 millions in August, and the demand for September promised to exceed £100 millions. The Bank held out to its last sovereign. It could pay no more. The gold standard was dead.

It was the British variant of the gold standard which died. The American variant lingered on for another eighteen months and then brought the United States to a financial and industrial collapse greater even than that which Britain had suffered. At the time of writing (November 1934) the French variant still lingers on. It is much more unsuitable to be the basis of an international currency than either the British or the American variants. But it is suited to the French psychology. It ministers to the European passion for hoarding. It is slowly, but surely, squeezing all the vitality out of the commercial and industrial life of Western Europe. What will be the outcome of the conflict between the passion for hoarding and the instinct for commercial and industrial progress it is at the moment impossible to say.

Britain withdrew herself from the crazy conflict

of three divergent gold standards in September 1931, and reverted to an inconvertible paper money currency. She had managed on an inconvertible paper currency with considerable success over a century previously (from 1797 to 1816). She had again managed an inconvertible paper currency from 1919 to 1924, the last two years of that period of management being marked with conspicuous success. In her relief from the intolerable oppression of a resuscitated gold standard, endured for a period of over six years, she naturally turned to her past success with an inconvertible paper currency in her search for a new currency standard, which would not expose her to the betrayal of her interests to which she had been exposed by her reliance on gold. It was but a few months after her withdrawal from the gold standard that Britain inaugurated a new currency system at Ottawa, notable in its detachment from gold as a possible basis for a stable international currency.

CHAPTER VII

THE AMERICAN COLLAPSE OF 1929

"The bank expansion resting on the policies of the Federal Reserve Banks, and resting on the inflowing gold that came to us because the rest of the world was off the gold standard and could not receive gold, amounted to $13\frac{1}{2}$ billion of deposits in the United States in the Commercial Banks and $14\frac{1}{2}$ billion in loans and investments, which we did not need.

"Commerce could not take it and would not use it, and it went into every other abnormal use which you can think of. It went into our vast foreign loans I speak about; it went into real estate and mortgage on a colossal scale.

"It went into instalment finance paper, rapidly growing and expanding; and it went into stock and bond collateral loans, and the banks investments in bonds, that wrecked so many banks when the market went to pieces in the last year or two."—Mr. BENJAMIN M. ANDERSON, Economist of the Chase National Bank, New York.

IT has already been explained in Chapter V that the constitution of the Federal Reserve System of currency control is widely different from the constitution of the Bank of England. There is a still greater discrepancy between the Banking System of the United States and that of Britain. The British Banking System comprises a small number of powerful banks, headed by what are known as "The Big Five." These five leading banks have branches in every town, every suburb, and in most of the large villages of the country. In addition there is a small number of other Joint Stock Banks, supplemented by a number (also very small) of merchant banks and discount, issue and acceptance houses. Though competing with each other, there is a high degree of unity and association in their methods of working, and a very close association with the Bank of England. The interest they give to depositors, and the interest they charge to borrowers of various classes of loans, are governed by the bank rate in accordance with a mutually agreed set of rules. Not only the banks, but the discount, issue and acceptance houses are continually in touch with the Bank of England. The relations with the Central Bank are friendly and cordial, but it is known that the Bank of England has behind it the power to force its policy on any individual bank that may prove recalcitrant. The British Banking System is an instance of perfect discipline producing perfect team work.

The American Banking System is almost the antithesis of the British System. It operates over a vaster expanse of country and on a much larger financial scale. It is, indeed, not one system but forty-eight State banking systems. The possibility of a unified branch banking system is not only precluded by geographical and political obstacles; it is negatived by law. It comprises some thousands of independent or unit banks, many of them not included in the Federal Reserve System. They compete with each other much more fiercely than British banks, and there is not the same degree of unity and association in their general methods of working. Each bank is a law to itself as to the rates of interest it charges, and there is no organic connection between local rates of interest and the bank rate. Quite apart from the lack of unity and control in the constitution and operations of the Federal Reserve Board itself, the banks of the American system have a freedom in their working that is not permitted to British banks.

The distinction between the two systems has been portrayed by Professor Luther A. Harr, of the University of Pennsylvania, in the following remarkable contrast:

The Governors of the Bank of England meet with the big heads of the five great banks operating in England, known as "The Big Five," which five banks do most of the commercial banking business there, together with the Chancellor of the Exchequer, and these seven men can make decisions that affect the entire English Banking System.

In the United States, to get a comparable degree of co-operation, it would be necessary to get together the Governors of the twelve Reserve Banks, the Federal Reserve Board, the Secretary of the Treasury, the Comptroller of the Currency, the heads of the forty-eight State Banking Systems, and some 14,000 Presidents of the Banks. Of course that presents a situation that makes unity of action impossible.

There is another difference between the two systems, which may seem merely a technical difference, but which is fundamental in the matter of the control exercised by the Central Body over the banking system. Banks which are members of the Federal Reserve System can always obtain currency from the Federal Reserve Banks by re-discounting the commercial bills they hold. British banks cannot obtain currency from the Bank of England so easily. They can only re-discount bills with the Bank of England in times of emergency, and then they have to pay dearly for the privilege. It is therefore much more easy for American banks to expand currency and to create bank money, in other words, to inflate, than it is for British banks.

Not only is the American banking system different from the British banking system in its lack of unity and homogeneity and its comparative freedom from central control, it is divergent in the nature of the banking business it performs for the public. The keynote of British banking is liquidity. The commercial paper it holds must be liquid; the securities it purchases must be readily convertible into currency, and the loans it sanctions must be of such a nature that their repayment at an early date is secured. The primary consideration of every loan issued is the capacity of the borrower to pay it back, quite irrespective of any collateral security he may have deposited. Similarly, the primary consideration in the purchase of any security is its immediate saleability should an emergency arise. Mortgage loans are regarded with grave suspicion, and issued only when there are means of payment in sight, apart from the property mortgaged. Loans for the purchase of securities are jealously limited to professional operators. The amateur speculator is severely discouraged. When collateral security is accepted, its earning power, rather than its market price, is the criterion of its security value.

The favourite forms of loan are a seasonal commercial loan, or a temporary loan for working capital, which can be repaid when the materials purchased by means of the loan have been worked up into a finished product and sold. Every bank tries to keep a high proportion of loans issued in this class. Of course mistakes are made; and these rules are in practice occasionally disregarded. But the standard of liquidity set is high, and the degree of attainment is not far short of the ideal prescribed.

So it is in the best American banks. But there were thousands of American banks, the great majority in fact, which fell to a lamentably low state of liquidity in the period 1927 to 1929. Very many banks, not only in remote towns and country districts, but also in large and important centres, had a dangerously high percentage of their loans on the mortgage of farms or real estate, or on the security of speculative bonds or shares. Many of their investments were in bonds and securities of very doubtful quality. Much of the collateral security they held, though valued at a substantial margin below market price, was over-valued with respect to its earning power. Many loans, issued nominally for short periods, or payable on demand, were allowed to run on indefinitely for years and years, as a mere matter of routine, without any warning or formal renewal. Amateur speculators were not drastically discouraged. And finally, a very unsafe proportion of loans was made for permanent capital expenditure.

The evidence to this effect is overwhelming. The quotation at the head of this chapter by one of the leading banker-economists of the United States indicates the generally unsatisfactory nature of the loans being issued before the collapse of 1929. It may be supplemented by a wide range of evidence of which the following are a few selections:

Dr. Willeford King, New York University:

Fairly slow assets, like mortgages and loans on stocks and bonds, increased tremendously in speculative times. There is where the danger lies.

Professor David Novick, New York University:

One of the great troubles with our banking system at the present time is that we have 90-day paper which has been in force five or ten years, and which was written with the idea that it would be in force five to ten years, when the note was first made. Paper that matures on long periods is not properly commercial banking paper.

Mr. A. W. Benkert, Chairman, Brookmere, Inc.:

The situation in 1929 was that a very large percentage of these loans, in many instances, were inadequately margined.

Mr. B. M. Anderson, Economist of the Chase National Bank:

The real estate mortgages of the members of the Federal Reserve Banks stood at 500 million dollars in 1919, and was over three billion dollars by 1928.

Mr. F. H. Vanderlip, formerly President of the National City Bank:

The very essence of banking is liquidity. There is no liquidity for a long term bond. It is a misapprehension about liquidity that wrecked our banking situation. Bankers received money payable on demand. They made loans on stocks and bonds. They made loans on real estate mortgages. Ultimately they came to own mortgages, that is, mortgage bonds of corporations. The ratio of self-liquidating paper began to drop as we organised corporations. The ratio gradually fell to a point where we had less than 30 per cent of self-liquidating commercial loans, and over 70 per cent of capital uses of our demand deposits.

Professor L. A. Harr, University of Pennsylvania:

What has our small banker been encouraged to make loans on in the past? Why, on real estate, on securities, then the so-called "commercial paper" which, in effect, in most cases is nothing but commercial paper. One may borrow on a thirty-day promissory note, expecting to pay the bank within the next ten years, but he really never has cash enough to pay at the maturity of the note.

When the Federal Reserve System was established in 1913, it was recognised that the control that would be exercised over the American banking system could not possibly be so strict a control as was exercised by the Bank of England over British banking. Yet there was one aspect of American banking that needed the strictest control possible. There was no law in Britain restricting the amount of bank money that could be created by the commercial banks. By a working arrangement between them and the Bank of England, it was limited to about ten times the total of their cash and their reserves with the Bank of England.

But such a working arrangement was impossible in the United States. It would be impossible for the

Federal Reserve Board to keep touch with the tens of thousands of banks, many of which did not belong to the Federal Reserve System. Moreover, it was the small and remote banks which tended to issue bank money in excess, and which were most in need of restraint. Consequently, the issue of bank money was limited by law. The reserves to be held varied from 7 to 13 per cent of demand deposits in accordance with the standing and location of the bank, and 3 per cent of time deposits.

A remarkable result followed. Though special care had been taken to differentiate the American regulation of the creation of bank money from the British method of regulation, the result in the aggregate amounted to the same in both countries. The amount of bank money created in both systems was approximately ten times the total of the cash and reserves of the commercial banks. The British system was voluntary; the American system was imposed by law. The British system was uniform for both time and demand deposits; the American system differentiated between them. The British proportion of ten to one was uniform for all banks and for all classes of deposits; the American proportion varied between 8 to 1 (13 per cent) and 33 to 1 (3 per cent). And yet, despite these differences, when the American system had settled down, it was found that the aggregate amount of bank money in circulation in America was approximately ten times the amount of cash and reserves of the commercial banks, exactly as in Britain.

This coincidence, though attention has frequently been drawn to it, has never been explained satisfactorily. It is probably due to an unconscious imitation of the old-established British proportion by the Federal Reserve Board. The commercial banks naturally attempt to press forward with their creation of bank money up to the limits permitted. The varied proportions in the United States would, if worked up to their limit, result in a much higher proportion than ten to one. But whenever that proportion was attained, the Federal Reserve Board, sensing danger if a higher aggregate proportion were permitted, began to adopt restrictive measures, and prevented it from passing that limit. The upward pressure of the commercial banks was continually trying to pass the ten to one proportion. The Federal Reserve System exercised a downward pressure whenever there was a danger of that proportion being exceeded. The result of these two opposing forces was a steady proportion of ten to one.

It is probable that this proportion of ten to one, adopted quite unconsciously, is the source of the American disasters of the last four years, monetary, financial and commercial. The creation of bank money on a ten to one proportion is perfectly safe in Britain. It is highly dangerous in the United States. Britain has voluntarily and consciously adopted it after an experience of over a century. The United States has adopted it unconsciously, after an experience of less than thirty years. In Britain it is operated by a highly experienced, closely associated, well disciplined, perfectly controlled banking system. In the United States it is operated by a banking system containing a very large element of inexperience. The system is highly individualistic and most divergent in its methods of working; its co-operative association is elementary; it is not disciplined into a unified system; and it is under imperfect control. In Britain the loans issued have a high degree of liquidity. In the United States, apart from a small proportion of the higher class banks, the contrary is the case.

All these considerations suggest that, whereas the creation of bank money on the basis of a proportion of ten to one is perfectly safe and feasible in Britain, it is risky and dangerous in the United States. But there is another criterion to be applied, quite apart from the differences of the banking systems of the two countries. The ten to one proportion of bank money in Britain has been built up on an experience of the currency psychology of the British people. The British people are free from the metallic complex, they have no inordinate faith in, nor reverence for, gold. They are completely indifferent about the convertibility of the internal currency. A high proportion of circulation of bank money is possible amongst a people so constituted.

But the currency psychology of the people of the United States is different. There is a very large proportion of people from the continent of Europe dwelling in the United States, and these have the metallic complex most highly developed. But, apart from these immigrants, the ordinary American has a very strong desire for the convertibility of his internal currency. Evidence to this effect is given in Chapter III. It may be further supplemented by:

Mr. RAND: We must have some co-ordination through the central authority that is perpetual, between the stock of money in this country, and the pieces of paper or forms of credit which are convertible into money, otherwise you do not have it convertible. When you get too far from convertibility it collapses. We are in a position where, if someone alarmed the public, or some event alarmed the public, the drop in price proceeding to an alarming extent, and people were afraid of their bank deposits not being convertible into cash, and rushing to the bank, where they are unable to get more than 10 per cent.

Mr. CROSS: People want to know that somewhere there is a redemption metal.

Dr. KING: Yes, that is true.

Mr. CROSS: I am talking from a psychological standpoint, you understand. We would have these fellows, especially from the Western States, having spasms.

Professor IRVING FISHER: I appreciate the fact that gold has a tradition that we have to take into account. It is embodied in our system, and, therefore, I accept the gold part as something that is necessary. I am willing to accept silver in the same way if it is politically necessary.

Mr. CROSS: Let me tell you about that political ground (the long-standing custom of using redemption metal); that is about 99 per cent of it in this country. You have got to touch the channels where the minds of people are, otherwise you will fall down in getting your bill through Congress.

Mr. BENKERT: He [Mr. Vanderlip] says these two latter, deposits and transactions, have grown to such proportions that the convertibility of paper into gold is impossible, because of the extent to which they have grown, and there-

fore the gold standard is unworkable. I think that is abso-
lutely true.

Mr. CROSS: The sociology of the country, and of Congress,
too, is so wedded to a metal base that you could not have
that bill passed unless you had it in the bill.

Mr. TUCKER: The people of the world, having been used
to gold and silver as the standard, gold and silver are the
only things they are now willing to take as the standard of
commodities.

The combination of a low degree of liquidity in the
banking system with a strong desire for convertibility
on the part of the public is a very dangerous combination. Bankers' money can circulate in Britain
to the extent of ten times the cash and reserves of
the commercial banks because Britain is free from
the desire for convertibility. But such a proportion
is dangerous in the United States. As Mr. Rand
states, if some event alarms the public, people are
afraid that their bank deposits are not convertible,
and if they rush to the banks they find that they are
only convertible up to 10 per cent.

Since the war there has been a still further difference between British and American conditions, which
makes the ten to one proportion dangerous for the
United States. The metallic basis of British currency
is a gold reserve at the Bank of England which never
departs far from the figure of £150 millions. But the
gold reserve for the Federal Reserve Board for the
past ten years has varied between £800 millions and
£1,000 millions (4,000 million dollars to 5,000 million
dollars). A ten to one superstructure of bank money

as currency based on the low figure of £150 millions of gold is not necessarily insecure. A ten to one super-structure of bank money as currency based on £1,000 millions of gold is almost certain to get beyond control.

The comparison of the American and British banking systems in the nature of the banking business undertaken, the wide disparity of their respective degrees of cohesion and unity, and in the different efficacy of the central control to which they are subjected, is essential to an understanding of the reasons why Governor Strong's policy of dollar stabilisation was adopted, and in due course abandoned, and why American prosperity collapsed in 1929.

The policy of dollar stabilisation was a purely internal policy. Its national character is best appreciated from the following statement by Mr. A. W. Benkert:

> We are not primarily interested in what is the relationship between the dollar and any other currency in the world. That is a matter of secondary interest. Ninety-three per cent of all the business in the United States is transacted between the people living within their own country. We are more concerned with the price level on goods and services we interchange within the United States than we are with the price level between the pound and the dollar. It is fundamentally so much more important that it is ridiculous for us to talk about the absolute necessity for stabilising exchange, so long as the price level has not been restored.

The case for Governor Strong's stabilisation policy against the traditional policy of the gold standard is therein stated as clearly and briefly as possible. But in actual practice it was found that the currency policy of the United States could not be managed independently of outside influences. The world price level had important and disturbing reactions on the dollar price level. These were not apparent as long as Britain continued the policy of the neutral pound, which she had maintained from 1922 to 1924. But when, in July 1924, Britain started a policy of severe deflation with a view to returning to the gold standard; and still more, after April 1925, when Britain had to continue its policy of severe deflation in order to maintain her position on the gold standard, that deflative policy operated with disturbing results on the efforts to stabilise the dollar. Governor Strong himself, before the Stabilisation Committee in 1926, formulated his difficulties in the following terms:

> There was taking place, and had for some little time taken place, a decline in the wholesale price level, and when we came to analyse that decline we found that it was almost entirely due to a decline in the prices of cotton and grains.

What was happening was that British deflation was lowering world wholesale price levels, and the prices of cotton and grains, being export commodities, were governed by world prices rather than by the purchasing power of the dollar. Deflation in world prices was hindering the stabilisation of dollar prices.

The dollar stabilisation policy had, in fact, to fight against four strong and intense forces:

   i. The traditional operation of the gold standard, which, on the basis of the unprecedentally large gold

    reserves accumulated in the United States, and the
    accepted ten to one proportion of bankers' money,
    tended to severe inflation;
  ii. The deflative policy of Britain, causing a severe
     decline in the world price level;
 iii. The limited powers of control possessed by the
     Federal Reserve System;
 iv. The lack of cohesion and unity in the American
     banking system.

The traditional operation of the gold standard is expressed in the previously quoted passage from the Macmillan Report:

> Countries which are receiving gold must be prepared to act on a policy which will have the effect of raising prices.

Now, if the Federal Reserve Board had possessed the unity and the controlling power of the Bank of England, and if the American banking system had been a united and disciplined team like the British banking system, it might have been possible to impose the revolutionary policy of stabilising prices against the traditional policy, which demanded the raising of prices. But in the circumstances a large section of the American banking system was hostile to the dollar stabilisation policy. They had tradition behind them. They had the whole weight of the orthodox gold standard behind them. They had the demands of the increased industrial activity of the country for additional currency behind them. However much the Federal Reserve Board might try, by sterilising the enormous reserves of gold flowing into the country, to adopt a policy of Reflation, the banking system of the country was creating bank money to the utmost extent of its capacity in the proportion of ten times its cash and reserves with the Federal Reserve Banks, and pressing with its whole force towards Inflation.

Another incalculable disturbing force now intervened. The wholesale Price Index of the United States is the weighted average of over seven hundred commodities entering into the ordinary consumption of the people. It includes both agricultural and industrial products. The British deflation commencing in 1924 operated to reduce the world price level of agricultural products. Such American commodities as wheat, cotton and meat products, which are exported, are governed by the world price level rather than by the purchasing power of the dollar. Consequently their prices were reduced and kept low by external currency forces.

This had a most unexpected effect on dollar stabilisation. The stabilisation of the dollar was being effected by keeping the general price level on the Wholesale Price Index as stable as possible. But the general price level was an average of the prices of over seven hundred commodities both agricultural and industrial. As the agricultural prices were pulled down by the world price level, the industrial prices had to go up to keep the average at a stable level. The dollar stabilisation policy therefore did not produce an even stimulating reflation throughout the country. Disturbed by the reactions of the world price level, it produced deflation in agriculture and inflation in industry. The reflation produced was not uniform. It was a compound of deflation over part of the country, the agricultural districts; and of inflation over the rest of the country, the industrial districts.

Despite these obstacles and unforeseen reactions the policy of the stabilised dollar achieved a remarkable measure of success. American industry prospered as it had never prospered before. Although agriculture did not share this prosperity, the increased purchasing power of the industrial part of the country mitigated to some extent the depressing effect of world agricultural prices. But dollar stabilisation did not achieve the stability of industry anticipated by its supporters. It had induced an industrial inflation. This inflation, though small at first, caused a tendency to speculation which alarmed the Federal Reserve Bank in 1927. The alarm grew to consternation in 1928. Ill-health had by this time forced Governor Strong to relinquish control of the operations of the Federal Reserve Board. In his absence the discontented and opposing elements asserted their influence, the dollar stabilisation policy was abandoned, and a return to the traditional gold standard was effected.

In place of the orderly operation of the dollar stabilisation process the return to the traditional gold standard produced a chaos of conflicting policies. Professor Irving Fisher, the most eminent economist in the United States, thus describes the confusion:

For political reasons, twelve regional banks were created in 1913 instead of one Central Bank. Only a loose and ineffective co-ordination was attempted through the Federal Reserve Board. The result has been chaos and internal dissension. The late Governor Strong tried to remedy this defect by inducing under his Chairmanship the governors of the four other largest banks, to form with him an Open Market Committee. At first it functioned well and we enjoyed a stable dollar for several years. But it soon resulted in a fight with the Federal Reserve Board, which abolished the self-appointed committee and superseded it with more cumbersome and inefficient machinery.

Had not such fatuous action been taken by the Federal Reserve Board, it is possible—in fact, I believe, probable —that this depression would have been a mild one. Its seriousness was due to the mismanagement of the Federal Reserve System. Such mismanagement could not be avoided so long as it was a house divided against itself.

Much the same testimony has been given by Professor Harr:

The tragic security inflation of 1927–29 could have been prevented if we had possessed a well-managed, unified, central banking system; but the inability of the Federal Reserve authorities to agree upon a policy, combined with the weakness and lack of courage of the members of the Federal Reserve Board, made it possible to have the security markets get out of control of the banking authorities.

Professor Novick also testifies:

As revealed in the Report [of the Federal Reserve Board] of 1928, you get a conflict in the Annual Report and in the Periodical Report, and a conflict between the Report of the Board and the reports of the districts.

In the confusion and chaos that prevailed the inflation that was causing the rapid increase of speculation was attributed to Governor Strong's dollar stabilisation policy. It was overlooked that Governor Strong had protected the United States for six years from the inflation, which the traditional operation of the gold standard on the enormous volume of gold reserves accumulated would have produced. It was overlooked that the gold reserves which Governor Strong had sterilised were still in the vaults of the Federal Reserve Banks, and that, if utilised, they would produce an immense inflative force. It was overlooked that a return to the traditional gold standard would mean the adoption of an inflation policy by the United States up to the limit permissible by the accepted proportion of ten times the cash and reserves of the commercial banks, which were themselves inflated by the release of the accumulated gold reserves.

It took over six years (April 1925 to September 1931) for the traditional gold standard to bring Britain to its knees. It took less than two years after the restraining policy of Governor Strong had ceased to operate for it to bring collapse and disaster to the United States. The dollar stabilisation policy was gradually abandoned, and a move towards the traditional gold standard policy was made in February 1928. In that month the bank rate was put up to 4 per cent, and it was further raised by two successive stages to 5 per cent by July 1928. The policy of reflation was dropped. The policy of deflation, by raising the bank rate, was adopted.

But although the Federal Reserve Board officially adopted the policy of deflation, it quite overlooked the inflative possibilities of the gold which had so far been sterilised by Governor Strong, and which was gradually being released for active use by the abandonment of his policy. This is clearly stated by Professor Novick in the words:

In a large measure, this 1927–29 rise was not the result of business activity, but was rather an artificial rise resulted from the release of gold impounded in the 1922–27 period.

The degree of inflation rendered possible by the release of this sterilised or impounded gold may be gathered from the following passages:

Mr. HANCOCK: I understand that beginning with 1922, excess reserves amounted to 300 millions, and between 1922 and 1928 the record shows deposits of banks increased $13\frac{1}{2}$ billions and loans increased $14\frac{1}{2}$ billions. To-day (1934) we have three times what we had in 1922 in reserves. What are the possibilities under the present set-up?

Professor HARR: To use those figures, I suppose one could say the extreme levels would be twenty times the excess reserve.

Also:

Mr. HANCOCK: The printed money, including check money and credit money, will run sometimes ten or fifteen, or even twenty times the amount of the actual currency?

Mr. B. M. ANDERSON: Yes.

It will be seen that the descriptions of Professors Fisher and Harr as to the state of chaos and confusion in the Federal Reserve Board are not overstated. The Board was acting on the Biblical injunction: Let not thy left hand know what thy right hand doeth. With its right hand it was imposing severe deflative measures by increasing the bank rate up to 4, 4½, and 5 per cent. With its left hand it was letting loose the inflative force of the impounded gold of the dollar stabilisation policy. It was both inflating and deflating. Its right hand was strangling industry. Its left hand was stimulating speculation. It was permitting the banking system to inflate up to the limits allowed by the enormous gold reserves. It was at the same time trying to control this inflation by raising the bank rate.

The results on the country were as chaotic and contradictory as the policy pursued. The inflation added fuel to the speculation that raged. The deflation effectually killed the prosperity of the country. As stated in the quotation at the head of this chapter, with respect to the inflated currency put into circulation:

> Commerce would not take it and would not use it, and it went into every other abnormal use you can think of.

From the national policy of stabilising the dollar, the Federal Reserve Board turned over to the international policy of the traditional gold standard, and co-operated with Britain and France in the deflation and restriction of credit which was depressing world prices and driving the countries and states producing primary commodities into despair, default and bankruptcy. Though credit was overflowing in the United States, industry had no use for it at the artificially high rates at which it could be obtained, based on a bank rate of 5 per cent. The disruptive forces, so graphically described in the Cunliffe Report of 1918 (see Chapter IV) began to operate. American prosperity, based on a 3½ per cent bank rate, began to wilt under the influence of a 5 per cent bank rate. A distinct slackening of industry was perceptible in the early months of 1929, and by the summer of that year depression had fastened on the country.

The contradictory policy of the Federal Reserve Board had resulted in the paradox that bank money was available in immense quantities, but at such a high rate of interest that it was useless for commercial and industrial purposes. That the over-issue of bank money under the normal operation of the gold standard created widespread concern is clear from the following evidence:

Mr. VANDERLIP: Remember that 1,000,000,000 dollars of gold may be multiplied into sixteen times that demand on your bank loans.

Professor IRVING FISHER: What we need to go after, ultimately, is a drastic improvement in our banking system whereby the issuance of credit is put on a safe basis by legislation. . . . We have allowed the private bankers to issue money whenever they allowed a man to borrow on his assets.

Mr. BUSBY: I don't believe that any sort of set-up which would permit the issuance of loans by banks, which loans become checking accounts, and therefore a type of bank currency, and therefore a part of the media of exchange in this country, will prove satisfactory unless there is a very adequate control of the amount of the bank currency which may be put out by the banking systems of this country. We must deal very drastically with that element, since it is nine-tenths of the media of exchange, and that nine-tenths can easily absorb the one-tenth which is coin and currency.

Mr. RAND: We should learn a lesson from the experience of the past ten years, during which we went through a terrific inflation of bank deposits.

Professor NOVICK: Both the re-discount policy and the open market policy failed to limit or affect the lending banks' lending policy.

Professor HARR: What I am interested in is a plan that will prevent the whole banking structure from carrying us into periods of inflation through the issuance of bank-cheque money, at times when we do not need it. No country uses so much bank-cheque currency as the United States. The gold supply in the United States is so much greater than we need to support the amount of cash in circulation and also the amount of bank credit.

The situation in the United States at the commencement of 1929 was, briefly, that commerce and industry were beginning to feel the adverse effects of the higher rates of interest, but that there were unlimited supplies of bank money available for any purpose that could afford to pay the higher rates demanded. The results were obvious. Commerce and industry declined; speculation flourished.

The speculation against which the deflative policy of the Federal Reserve Board was aimed had commenced in a perfectly legitimate manner. Commercial prosperity had placed large numbers of people in the position that they had savings to invest. They invested them in the ordinary course of events in the securities they considered would give them the best dividends on their money. But the mild industrial inflation under the dollar stabilisation policy, to which attention has been drawn, tended to send up the price of the securities purchased. The new investors found that the appreciation of the value of the securities was a source of profit they had not anticipated. They were gradually and insidiously drawn into speculation as an exciting and a remunerative hobby, much more interesting and profitable than sitting quietly and drawing small quarterly dividends.

Instead of discouraging these amateur speculators, the banks were only too pleased to find a profitable outlet for their surplus bank money, for which there was a slackening demand for commercial purposes. Advances were made at fairly high rates, and were secured at what were deemed to be ample margins on the value of the collateral security deposited. When the dollar stabilisation policy was abandoned, and the amount of bank money greatly increased by the release of the previously impounded gold, speculation was greatly encouraged. The higher rates of interest imposed by the Federal Reserve Board, though strongly deterrent to trade and industry, had no effect whatever on speculation. They stimulated speculation rather than discouraged it. The bankers, having large supplies of bank money, which could not be loaned to commerce and industry owing to the high rates of interest demanded, permitted them to be used for speculation.

The surplus bank money available was not confined to Stock Exchange speculations. It was utilised for speculation in real estate, and also in speculative building construction. The banking system was undoubtedly responsible for the beginning of the speculation fever in all its forms; but in 1928 there was a remarkable development which took control of speculation entirely out of the hands of the banking system.

The prices of securities on any Stock Exchange are regulated by the balance of opinion between the bulls and the bears. The bulls think prices will rise, and so buy shares. The bears think prices will fall, and so sell them. Every Stock Exchange transaction is between a bull and a bear. The purchaser is a bull, and the seller is a bear. There are also a large number of passive bears, who keep the prices of shares down by refraining from buying shares, and keeping their money in deposit, thinking that the tendency will be for shares to fall.

In 1927 the balance between the bulls and the bears was upset by the irruption of a large number of amateur bulls, or new investors, into the market. They kept bringing extra funds into the market and sending prices up. Normally, the bears restore the balance by selling their shares at the higher prices obtainable, and taking the proceeds out of the market. The amount of money taken out of the market ordinarily equals the amount of money brought into the market, and prices again become stable.

But in 1927, and still more in 1928, the amount of money coming into the market was so great that it was constantly in excess of the amount abstracted by the sales of the bears. The amount was much greater than the sums put into the market by the new amateur speculators. In due course the source of this extra money supporting and raising the prices of shares in the market was ascertained. The bears, when they sold their stocks, did not place their money into deposit. They lent it on call (that is, payable back at a moment's notice) at a high rate of interest to the stockbrokers. The stockbrokers advanced it, in the ordinary course of business, to the purchasers of shares on part payment.

The bears, therefore, instead of standing up against the bulls, and keeping share prices down, were supplying the bulls in an indirect manner with the ammunition to keep share prices up. This explains the prolonged and obstinate nature of the speculation which started to gather force from 1927 and culminated in 1929. It was fed from three sources:

i. The surplus bank money created on the release of the gold previously sterilised under the dollar stabilisation policy.
ii. The large number of amateur speculators attracted into the Stock Exchange by the continuous rise of securities due to such inflation.
iii. The return of bear money, released by the sale of securities, through the brokers, into the market.

The efforts of the Federal Reserve Board to stop speculation by raising the Bank Rate only served to increase its intensity. The Macmillan Report describes the situation as follows:

The Reserve System tried to check the rising flood of speculation by moral suasion and by bringing pressure to bear upon the New York member banks, hoping thereby to cut off the supply of call loan money to the Stock Exchange at the source. But though the supply of call-money from the New York banks was successfully cut off, the total volume of call-money continued to rise.

When the brokers found they could not get the money they needed from the banks, they offered extravagant rates of interest to the bears who had sold their securities. In the spring of 1929 the call rate of interest actually exceeded 20 per cent. By October 1929 the amount of money lent to the New York stockbrokers by the banks was exceeded by the amount they had obtained from other sources, that is, from the bears. The banks' advances were under 3,000,000,000 dollars. The advances from other sources were, approximately, 4,000,000,000 dollars. How this amount was attained is thus explained in the Macmillan Report:

There was thus drawn into the vortex of American specu-lation a mass of short money, not only from non-banking agencies in the United States, but from European countries as well; though, as regards European funds, the bulk came from deposits previously made in the United States.

The best account of the actual collapse is given by Mr. B. M. Anderson in the following terms:

This one thing I want to tell you happened in the Chase Bank in that panic week. At the beginning of that panic week, October 22, 1929, we had loaned of our own money at the money post of the Stock Exchange, only 225,000 dollars. We did not like the situation. But we were lending, for the account of others, vast sums, not at our instance, but on their instructions; that is, if a customer told us to do a thing, it is our business to do it. We were lending money for country banks and others, great corporations, private investors, foreign banks, who instructed us to debit their account and lend on call. In the week that followed we got calls from these people. They did not wish to telegraph or write, but they called by 'phone at the bank, and said, "Call our money." We called it.

There is the story of the collapse in a nutshell. The Chase National Bank had only a trifle lent to the Stock Exchange. But its customers had lent millions of dollars on call at high rates to the stockbrokers. So had the customers of other banks. The total amount so lent amounted approximately to 4,000,000,000 dollars. In the week succeeding October 22, 1929, the customers of the Chase National Bank, in a panic, 'phoned to the bank to call in their money. So did the customers of the other New York banks. The Chase National Bank promptly called in its share of the 4,000,000,000 dollars. The other New York banks called in the remainder. The Stock Exchange was totally unable to respond to a demand for the return of four billion dollars at a moment's notice, and collapsed.

Mr. Busby, Member of the House of Representatives for Mississippi, has given another account of the collapse, which closely tallies with that of Mr. Anderson. He states:

When the crash started, 56 per cent of call loans outstanding had been made for the account of others, and within a few days all of that $3\frac{1}{2}$ billion dollars that had supported, or helped to support, the Stock Market, was withdrawn.

The descriptions of Messrs. Anderson and Busby regarding the collapse of October 1929 are deficient in one particular. They do not state why there should have been such a universal panic in the week succeeding October 22, 1929, leading to the withdrawal from the Stock Exchange of the call money advanced from other sources than the New York banks amounting to 4 billion dollars. The cause of the panic is, however, obvious. American prosperity had been checked in the spring of 1929. In the summer the retardation of prosperity, from being slight, and possibly only temporary, began to assume serious proportions. A further rise of the bank rate to 6 per cent in August 1929 put the matter beyond all doubt. The phase of bounding prosperity was at an end, and a period of difficulty lay ahead.

The news that prosperity, the goose which had been laying the golden eggs, if not killed, was temporarily incapacitated, began to filter abroad. Those in the know withdrew their money from the stock-brokers while they could get it. But such knowledge could not be kept concealed from the public for long. The trickle of withdrawals became a stream, a river, a raging torrent, in the course of two months. Everybody withdrew because everybody else was withdrawing. The knowledge that American prosperity was declining to a level which would not support the inflated values to which securities had climbed, caused a panic, and the panic caused the collapse.

The narrative here given of the circumstances leading to the American collapse of 1929 is not that usually presented to British readers. The customary version follows broadly the sequence that the departure of the United States from the strict orthodoxy of the gold standard in 1922 led to inflation; inflation led to speculation; speculation led to financial collapse; and financial collapse caused the decline in prosperity. This version is so completely contrary to the facts that great care has been taken in presenting a narrative more in accordance with the real causation and sequence of events. The above version is incorrect in the following particulars:

Inflation was due to the operation of the traditional gold standard acting on an abnormal accumulation of gold reserves.

The departure of the United States from the strict orthodoxy of the gold standard, instead of causing inflation, kept inflation at bay for six years, from 1922 to 1928.

The outburst of speculation was due to the operation of the traditional gold standard acting on the excess gold reserves when released from the sterilisation imposed upon them by the dollar stabilisation policy, and thereby causing a severe inflation of currency and credit, but at prices too high for commerce and industry to benefit.

The decline in prosperity preceded the collapse in speculation, and was not caused by that collapse. Speculation collapsed because of the decline in prosperity.

The decline in prosperity was due to the deflative effect of the rise of the bank rate from $3\frac{1}{2}$ to 5 per cent and subsequently to 6 per cent; rates too high for commerce and industry, which followed the sequence outlined in the Cunliffe Report of 1918 as resulting from a rise in the bank rate.

It is not only in Britain that the causes of the collapse of 1929 are imperfectly understood. They are but imperfectly understood in the United States. The period of uncertainty and depression between 1929 and 1933 has tended to distract attention from the memorable achievement of the dollar stabilisation policy. Against almost insuperable obstacles, it brought the United States to the highest level of prosperity it has yet achieved. Its abandonment reduced the nation to unprecedented depths of despair and depression. But, though temporarily eclipsed, its success while it lasted was too outstanding to be lightly put aside and forgotten. It pointed the way to permanent and universal currency reform. It proved that the proposals of the Genoa Conference of 1922 were not dreams, but were capable of realisation. The spirit of the dollar stabilisation policy was shortly to be revived in an unexpected quarter, the Report of the British Macmillan Commission on Banking and Currency.

CHAPTER VIII

THE MACMILLAN REPORT

"Such a proposal (the proposal of the Macmillan Report to secure a stable average level for wholesale world prices) really means the substitution of an Index Figure for gold as the standard of value, and the new unit of value would, if the proposal were adopted, be better represented by a counter to be issued by a trustworthy international authority. The world would then be saved the labour and expense of gold-mining, and the Central Banks the worry of having perpetually to devise expedients to adjust the value of that no longer necessary commodity to the value of the new unit.

"I doubt whether the proposal will come within the range of practical politics during the lifetime of the youngest of us."—LORD BRADBURY

THE above passage shows Lord Bradbury at his best and at his worst. It would be difficult to improve upon his masterly analysis of the essence of the proposals of the Macmillan Report. In a few pungent phrases he tore away the veil of camouflage and diplomacy with which the real proposals had been concealed. "The substitution of an Index Figure for gold as the standard of value"; "gold a no longer necessary commodity"; "the new unit of value a counter issued by a trustworthy international authority"; these, and not the pretended retention of the gold standard, were the true recommendations of the Report.

But how remote from reality did Lord Bradbury prove himself to be when, in his contempt, he relegated

their consideration to a period beyond the lifetime of
the youngest of us. Within three months of the publication of his prophecy, they were vital issues, the
predominant issues in the world of currency and
finance; within fifteen months they had been adopted
as the official currency policy of the British Commonwealth; within two years they had bound together
a League of Nations prepared to follow a sterling
currency operated on them as foundations. Scarcely
two years from the prophecy of Lord Bradbury had
elapsed, when the proposals he had so contemptuously
dismissed, embodied in the Ottawa Currency Policy,
were made the objective of a determined combined
attack by the City of London, under the leadership
of Mr. Montagu Norman, *The Times*, and the French
Delegation to the World Economic Conference. That
triple attack was routed by the mere exposition by
President Roosevelt of the principles enumerated in
the Macmillan Report and dismissed with such
contempt by Lord Bradbury. This was a healthy record
of achievements in two years for a proposal that would
not "come within the range of practical politics during
the lifetime of the youngest of us."

The Macmillan Commission was appointed on
November 5, 1929, exactly a fortnight after the sensa-
tional collapse in the United States had commenced
to develop. Its terms of reference were:

To enquire into banking, finance and credit, paying
regard to the factors both internal and international which
govern their operation, and to make recommendations

calculated to enable these agencies to promote the development of trade and commerce, and the employment of labour.

The Report was issued to Parliament in June 1931, at a time when Britain was in the throes of a desperate financial crisis. British industry and commerce had been in a state of acute and deepening depression for seven years. Unemployment was steadily mounting towards the dreaded figure of 3,000,000. Exports had declined to half their previous value. Receipts from such invisible exports as interest on foreign securities, and payments for banking, shipping and insurance services to the rest of the world, had seriously declined. For the first time for over a century Britain experienced an adverse Balance of Trade. The Budget was unbalanced. A financial panic on the continent of Europe had frozen the short-term credits on which the solvency of the London Money Market depended. And, to crown all, just as London's liquid assets were frozen stiff, an unprecedented drain on the gold of the Bank of England was being caused by the renewal of continental hoarding on a wholesale scale.

Drastic revolutionary action was necessary to meet such a combination of adverse circumstances. But drastic and revolutionary proposals would have intensified the panic on the Continent, and destroyed confidence in Britain's capacity to pull the world out of the slough of depression into which it had fallen. There was no panic in Britain. There was no distrust of Britain on the Continent. What the Continent wanted was gold, gold, gold. In a world where everything else was depreciating, gold was the only thing that was appreciating in value. The Continent turned to London to satisfy its craving for gold. The only doubts were whether, in view of the large accumulations of gold by the Central Banks of France and the United States, London would be able to supply a sufficient quantity of gold to satisfy the continental craving for it.

The majority of the Members of the Macmillan Commission knew that the historic gold standard was dead. They knew that three conflicting systems of currency, each under the deceptive name of "the gold standard," were operating in Britain, France, and the United States respectively. They knew that a revolutionary "cut adrift" from the paralysing effects of an obsolete system of currency was imperative. They knew that the situation was so critical that they recorded:

it may be that the whole machine may crack before reaction back to equilibrium has been brought about.

That was their great fear—that the whole machine might crack. Consequently, though they embodied in their report revolutionary proposals of a drastic nature, they clothed them in such diplomatic language that their import would be only gradually realised. They wished to reassure the public that all was for the best in the best of all possible worlds. They succeeded beyond their expectations. The Macmillan Report was regarded as demonstrating that whoever was to blame, Britain had nothing with which to reproach herself. The prevalent impression was that the Macmillan Report had recommended that nothing could go really wrong so long as Britain adhered to that effective safeguard against all monetary ills—the gold standard.

It was a great feat. To demonstrate that the historic gold standard was dead and buried beyond all hope of resurrection, and yet to recommend it as the only possible basis for a new and reformed system of currency, needed the exercise of considerable diplomacy. To present the conflicting operation of three essentially divergent gold standards as being "joint and several efforts to secure stability" required more than diplomacy. To make the rejected proposals of the Genoa Conference of 1922 the basis of their recommendations camouflaged revolution under a cloak of tradition. To make practical proposals for stabilising both the world wholesale prices and the international exchanges, linked the revolution with the gold standard. To have expanded Governor Strong's dollar stabilisation policy into a recommendation for the stabilisation of world wholesale prices demonstrated that the revolutionary policy recommended was based on a practical experiment which had achieved remarkable success.

But the supreme achievement of the Macmillan Report was to propose that Britain should adopt a Price Index standard of currency, without anyone but Lord Bradbury (himself a member of the Commission) discerning the exact nature of the revolution proposed. His warning might have been effective if he had not ventured into the realms of prophecy. But nobody could be alarmed at a revolution which would not take effect "during the lifetime of the youngest of us."

The numerous passages from the Report, indicating that the historic gold standard had passed away, never to return, are scattered throughout its pages. Their language is elusive, and they are usually embedded so deeply in their context that quotation is difficult. Many of them are associated with the fact that participation with the United States and with France will prevent the renewal of anything resembling the pre-war gold standard. Among such passages are:

Among the causes of instability is the entry of the United States into the group of the chief creditor countries (which) has caused a dispersion of initiative and responsibility in the leadership of international finance.

Movements of gold have ceased of late to have what used to be considered their "normal" effect on the domestic credit policy of certain countries, notably France and the United States. In recent years it has been impossible to rely upon action being taken by both the country losing gold and the country gaining gold to preserve international equilibrium.

The difficulties have arisen through the partial failure of the two recipients (the United States and France), during the last two or three years, to employ receipts in the way in which Great Britain has always employed hers, namely, either in the purchase of additional imports or in making additional foreign loans on long terms. On the contrary, they have required payment of a large part of their annual surplus either in actual gold or in short-term liquid claims. This is a contingency which the normal working of the international gold standard does not contemplate and for which it does not provide.

The automatic working of the gold standard even then (pre-war) was more or less limited to the sphere of the Bank of England, and was satisfactory in its results only because London was then by far the most powerful centre in the world. But post-war conditions are widely different. In the first place, New York has risen to be an exceedingly powerful monetary centre with as strong a pull on the gold resources of the world as London.

We repeat that it is the simultaneous reluctance of creditor countries (France and the United States) either to lend or to buy which is the cause of the crisis.

In brief, the conceptions of the United States and France, as to the methods, the obligations, the responsibilities, and the objectives of the gold standard are so opposed to British conceptions that their participation in its management and control transformed it into something radically different from the pre-war gold standard. Or, in other words, the pre-war gold standard under British control was transformed into three distinctive post-war gold standards.

Another class of passages indicate the failure of the gold standard to cope with post-war conditions:

The working of the gold standard must be adjusted to these striking changes in world conditions, and the task of adjustment must be entrusted to the Central Banks.

It is not possible even for a creditor country to go far in the direction of increasing either its own buying or its own lending unless the other creditor countries are moving more or less in step.

Creditor countries must, unless they are ready to upset

the economic conditions, first of the debtor countries and then of themselves, be prepared to lend back their surplus instead of taking it in gold.

The effect of the operation of the gold standard in producing the deplorable conditions in which the debtor nations find themselves is repeatedly emphasised:

The position of the debtor countries is apt to deteriorate rather than to improve as a result of their having to export gold.

The debtor countries of the world will be the first to find the strain unbearable.

Whether the gold factor would, or would not, operate as a drag on the price level depends on the way in which the individual Central Banks were working the system, whether they were accumulating gold reserves greatly in excess of legal requirements.

It is a great misfortune for us and for the raw material countries that we should have a great volume of unemployment through their inability to purchase from us as the result of a fall in the price of their produce.

It is unlikely therefore that the debtor countries can continue much longer to square their international position by parting with gold at a rate of £70,000,000 a year, as they have been forced to do in the last two years.

The transformation of the pre-war gold standard into a standard of a totally different nature in its essence and in its methods of operation is described in numerous parts of the Report. A few selections will illustrate their purport:

The nineteenth-century philosophy of the gold standard was based on the assumptions. . . . But in the modern post-war world neither of these assumptions is invariably valid.

Formerly it was assumed that the efflux and influx of gold itself produced a new equilibrium. . . . In actual fact to-day . . . when equilibrium is profoundly upset between creditor and debtor nations, the whole world suffers.

According to the classical theory of the gold standard, the same result should ensue. . . . But, in the modern world . . . it may be that the whole machine will crack before the reaction back to equilibrium has been brought about.

All Central Banks are faced with the necessity of a greater "management" of their currency systems.

Full quotations have not been given, partly because the passages from which they are taken are lengthy, and partly because the object of the quotations is to illustrate the antithesis between the pre-war and post-war gold standards. This is effected by the complementary phrases:

The nineteenth-century philosophy of the gold standard, and—in the modern post-war world.
Formerly, and—in actual fact to-day.
According to the classical theory of the gold standard, and—But in the modern world.

These antithetical phrases could only be used to indicate fundamental distinctions.

The probable and immanent disintegration of the gold standard is foreshadowed in such passages as:

Should it not prove so, we can scarcely expect the international gold standard to survive in its present form.
Naturally, the total result leads some people to question the desirability of adhering to an international standard.
Many countries, both to-day and at former times, have found that such continual adherence (to an international standard) involves a strain greater than they can bear.
We fear that many Central Banks, being anxious concern-

145   K

ing the adequacy of their gold reserves, will be in constant danger of nipping off a renewal of confidence, of causing a premature reaction of activity, and of ultimately dragging down prices below the level which we have indicated as desirable.

Failing this the creditor countries will soon have sucked all the gold available in the hands of the debtor countries, and this may entail a series of defaults.

Further quotations appear to be unnecessary. The two last are the most damaging of all. A currency standard which impels Central Banks to nip off a renewal of confidence, to cause a premature reaction of activity, and to drag and keep down prices; and which sucks the gold of the debtor countries till they are driven to default, is condemned beyond all hope of reprieve. The massed effect of these quotations was lost through their being scattered widely throughout the Report, and buried in their context. Moreover, their effect was neutralised by such comforting passages as:

Nevertheless, the violent movements of the post-war period are no doubt exceptional, and, while we cannot hope that they are yet at an end, we may reasonably look for a gradual improvement.

We have recommended that the country should continue to adhere to the international gold standard at the existing parity.

There can be little or no hope of progress at an early date for the monetary system of the world as a whole, except as the result of a process of evolution starting from the historic gold standard.

The next phase of monetary policy must consist of a wholehearted attempt to make the existing international standard work more satisfactorily.

Experience does not show that a creditor country with a diversified trade is liable to suffer undue domestic strain merely as the result of adherence to an international standard.

However, though the gold standard was to be maintained, a very well planned line of retreat from the gold standard to a Price Index standard was mapped out, with complete direction posts:

The international gold standard can, under appropriate conditions, enable both exchange stability and a considerable degree of price stability to be attained simultaneously over a wide area.

It may be considered a secondary object of the international gold standard to preserve a reasonable stability of international prices.

A failure by the Central Banks to attempt to redress the fall in prices, in our judgment, would endanger the principles on which modern economic society is founded.

The major objectives of a sound monetary policy—the maintenance of the parity of foreign exchanges, the avoidance of the credit cycle, and the stability of the price level. . . .

Are we justified in supposing that comparative stability of international prices can be achieved by a wise and concerted policy on the part of the central banks?

The function of a Central Bank should be to regulate the volume and price of bank credit, so as to maintain output and employment at the maximum compatible with adherence to the gold standard and with maintenance of the stability of the international price level.

At present any deliberate effort at stability (of prices), however crude in its methods and partial in its success, would be a great improvement.

The objective of raising the international price level would probably command widespread though not universal approval.

The aim of the Central Banks should be to maintain the stability of international prices.

On the vexed questions as to the degree to which the price level is, and can be, and should be, controlled by monetary policy, the Macmillan Report states definitely:

The recent world-wide fall in prices is best described as a monetary phenomenon, which has occurred as the result of the monetary system failing to solve successfully a problem of unprecedented difficulty and complexity.

The Credit Cycle seems to be the effect of monetary conditions upon human psychology.

It should be our object to increase the power to exercise deliberate control over the price level, that there is nothing inherently impracticable in this.

The degree to which the price level remains stable over a period of time is again profoundly influenced by policy.

What can emphatically be said is, that instability of prices is a serious evil, that monetary influences on prices are more controllable than any other, and that the Central Banks should therefore so control such monetary influences as to favour stability rather than instability.

Stability (of prices) over short periods, or in other words, the mitigation so far as possible, of the Credit Cycle, is, we believe, largely a question of co-operative currency management.

Thus, the gold standard failed to solve the post-war problems of unprecedented difficulty and complexity. But such problems must be faced. The world is not at the mercy of incalculable forces creating boom and slump, prosperity and depression. The operating forces are controllable, and must be controlled. Previously the solution of the problems—

required a degree of knowledge, experience and prescience, which no one in fact possessed, or could have been expected to possess.

But that is no reason for running away from them now. We have greater knowledge and greater experience, and, though we may not have greater prescience, we at least know the direction in which the solution is to be found. It is to be found in the substitution of a scientific currency standard based on a Price Index, instead of being based on one commodity, gold, which has recently developed the dangerous characteristic of being highly unstable in value. Lord Bradbury's critical description of the essence of the Macmillan Report will be found to be fully justified by the following passages:

> We mean by the international price level in this context, the composite price at wholesale of the principal foodstuffs and raw materials entering into international trade as measured by the best-known wholesale Index Numbers.
> The ultimate aim should be the stability of the international price level, meaning by this the composite price at wholesale of the principal foodstuffs and raw materials entering into international trade as measured by the best-known wholesale Index Numbers.

The repetition of this definition (it occurs in paragraphs 266 and 300) indicates the stress laid by the members of the Commission on the fact that the international price level is to be closely associated with an Index Number. The price level is, in fact, to be "measured" by an Index Number. The standard of measurement is to be an Index Number, not gold. The following passages must be read with the knowledge that whenever the term "international price level" is used, it implies measurement by means of a Price Index standard:

> We have recommended that after prices have been raised sufficiently, we should aim at maintaining the stability of prices at the higher level thus reached.
>
> Our objective should be, so far as it lies within the power of this country, to influence the international price level, first of all to raise prices a long way above the present level, and then to maintain them at the level thus reached, with as much stability as can be managed.
>
> A large rise towards the price level of 1928 is greatly to be desired.
>
> The main objective of the Central Banks, acting in co-operation in the management of the international gold standard, should be to maintain the stability of international prices both over long periods and over short periods.
>
> The method by which the Central Banks must attempt to achieve their aim of maintaining stability of the international price level over long and short periods is through the control of the volume and terms of bank credit.

Lord Bradbury was the only member of the Macmillan Commission to dissent from its Report. His able defence of the gold standard in his Memorandum of Dissent is particularly interesting, because no man in Britain has done more than Lord Bradbury to facilitate Britain's withdrawal from the gold standard, and to demonstrate that the gold standard is both unnecessary and obsolete. He was the high Treasury Official whose signature guaranteed British currency notes during the war. His name was in the pocket of every British citizen possessing a ten-shilling note. All slang terms for the higher forms of currency vanished during the war in favour of "Bradburies." It was not a term of disapproval. It was rather one of affection, mixed with wonder and awe at the power of a man whose mere signature could create money to the extent of hundreds of millions of pounds.

The unquestioned and unconcerned acceptance of Bradburies proved to be a "very present help in time of trouble" to the British currency authorities at the conclusion of the war. They dreaded the demand for convertibility. But the demand never came. Whether at war, or in time of peace, the British citizen proved to be completely indifferent whether his pound note was convertible into gold or not. With immense feelings of relief the Bank of England recognised that the British people themselves had solved the most difficult of all currency problems—that of managing their internal transactions without the intervention of gold. The magic of the name "Bradbury" had proved superior to the magic of gold. Henceforth, whatever currency troubles might arise, paper, managed on commonsense lines, would suffice for the entire internal monetary transactions of Britain. Gold could be reserved entirely for international use.

It was a supreme stroke of irony that made the name of this staunch defender of the gold standard a practical proof that gold is superfluous for currency purposes. His attitude towards currency is best exemplified by the following extract from his Memorandum of Dissent:

If currency "management" is to be used to facilitate currency movements of this type (stimulating capital development by means of loans) the sooner we return to an "automatic" system the better. Honesty, even if stupid, is a better foundation for credit than the most adroit finesse.

Nevertheless, his Memorandum of Dissent is a valuable document. It tore away the concealing veils of camouflage and diplomacy from the Macmillan Report. In derision it placed the red cap of revolution upon its head, and exhibited it to the public as it really was, *sans culotte.*

Neither the Report nor the Memorandum of Dissent attracted more than momentary notice. The late Mr. F. C. Goodenough, Chairman of Barclays Bank, delivered a denunciatory address to the Institute of Actuaries. He approved Lord Bradbury's Memorandum of Dissent, and strongly disapproved all managed currencies, but admitted that a managed currency would be a necessity for Britain for the time being. He enumerated a number of obstacles that would prevent an early return to the gold standard. Like Lord Bradbury he ventured into realms of prophecy, with equally disastrous results. He stated that he felt sure—

that a purely managed currency would not appeal to the Dominions or Colonies as a suitable system.

A few months subsequently the Dominions were assisting in the establishment of a purely managed currency at Ottawa.

All the elaborate precautions taken by the Macmillan Commission to conceal the revolutionary nature of the proposals were in vain. Events were moving rapidly to a crisis. Australia and New Zealand had already left the gold standard. The hoarders of gold on the Continent were draining the Bank of England to its last sovereign. The hoarding value of gold completely dominated its currency value. Britain withdrew from the gold standard three months after the Report was published.

With the withdrawal of Britain from the gold standard the Macmillan Report was immensely simplified. All the elaborate subterfuges by which the gold standard was to be transformed into a price-index standard were unnecessary. The gold standard was dead so far as Britain was concerned. Everything in the Report appertaining to the gold standard became so much dead wood ready for the pruning-knife. The dreaded "cut adrift" which had so alarmed the members of the Macmillan Commission had actually happened. Instead of producing doubt and despair, it had inspired exhilarating emotions of relief, freedom and confidence.

A short space of time to settle down after the exciting events of the summer of 1931 being allowed, the task of pruning the dead wood out of the Macmillan Report was entrusted to the Imperial Conference at Ottawa, due to meet in the summer of 1932. The Press reports made the Ottawa Conference appear to have been nothing more than a sordid wrangle over tariff concessions. But long after all memories of the tariff achievements of the Ottawa Conference have vanished, it will stand out in history as the instrument by which the recommendations of the Macmillan Report were translated into a practical form, and became the actively working currency system of the nations of the British Commonwealth in supersession of the vanished gold standard.

CHAPTER IX

THE OTTAWA CURRENCY REVOLUTION

It is no small thing to have obtained the unanimous consent of all the Empire Governments for the determination of the United Kingdom not to return to the gold standard until remedies have been found for the conditions which make it unworkable.

"It should reassure the many industrialists and others who have feared that attempts would be made to persuade Great Britain to return to the gold standard in circumstances which would make such return disastrous."—*The Times* Editorial on Ottawa, August 18, 1932.

WHETHER it was accident or design which selected Ottawa to be the birthplace of the currency system destined to supersede the gold standard, it was an excellent choice. In his evidence before the Macmillan Commission, Mr. Montagu Norman had drawn attention to a serious anomaly in the relations and locations of industry and finance in Britain:

Industry, mainly in the North; finance, mainly in the South.

A monetary conference held in London would have been highly susceptible to the financial atmosphere. At Ottawa the delegates were able to frame their policy free from the disturbing influences which helped to wreck the World Economic Conference twelve months later.

The feeling of detachment and freedom was heightened by the fact that the Canadian currency is on a dollar basis. The fate of the pound sterling was to be decided at a centre and in an environment where it was known only by repute and hearsay. At Ottawa the pound sterling was a remote abstraction, known only through its repercussions on the value and purchasing power of the dollar. It did not enter into the daily life and transactions of the country. Such a neutral environment was far more conducive to the emergence of a practical working policy than the hectic clangour which enveloped the World Economic Conference.

The credit for making the first suggestion which led to the inauguration of a new currency system must be awarded to the Federation of British Industries. In September 1931, on the eve of Britain's withdrawal from the gold standard, a Special Committee of the Federation issued a Report on Empire Monetary and Financial Policy, which contained the following proposals:

(1) An Empire Conference should be summoned to examine the practicability of establishing a stable Empire Currency system to link together the financial policies of constituent members of the British Empire on a basis of free co-operation.

Agreeing with the general analysis of the Macmillan Report as to the causes of the recent fall in prices and as to the disastrous character of its effects, the Committee are also in broad agreement with the one positive general conclusion of the report, which is that the raising of prices above their present level is an immediate necessity, and they declare their emphatic opinion that to allow prices to be stabilised at their present level—not to speak of a further fall—would be a serious disaster for all countries of the world alike.

As regards Empire currency co-operation, the Committee state that the British Empire is not in the political sense a unitary state. Any monetary unity that is attainable must be arrived at by free co-operation. The Committee, while admitting that the ideal solution would be a monetary system which secured for mankind generally a reasonable stability of prices and a measure of security against the disastrous sequence of alternate boom and depression, feel that, in the absence of sufficiently far-reaching international co-operation to effect such a purpose, the partner nations of the Empire should not neglect the opportunity afforded by the extent of their trade and resources to secure for themselves the benefits throughout the Empire of stable exchanges and of comparatively stable prices, and to give, by their success, an encouraging example to the world.

The establishment—over an economic unit of such magnitude as a developed British Empire might well become —of a single stable currency system would not only result in a very large economy of bullion and its liberation for world currency purposes; it would, in a large measure, tend to control the monetary value of the precious metals, and consequently of world currency generally. It is a good thing to have an ultimate goal to work towards, that goal, in the monetary sphere, might well be an Imperial sterling currency, so adjusted as to maintain reasonable price stability for the British Commonwealth, and so powerful as to govern, through the external trade of that Commonwealth, both the value of the metallic medium of exchange, and, indirectly, the value of the currencies of the rest of the world.

These proposals—the calling of an Empire Currency Conference; the utilisation of the Macmillan proposals as the basis of a new currency system; Empire currency co-operation as a step towards world currency

co-operation; price stability for the British Commonwealth as a step towards price stability for the world
as a whole—form a remarkable forecast of what
actually happened at Ottawa; as remarkable as the
forecast, made seven years previously, as to what
would happen if Britain returned to the gold standard.

The membership of the Monetary and Financial
Committee of the Ottawa Conference had exactly
that diversity of personalities and points of view that
tended to a broad-minded consideration of every
issue that would arise. Mr. Bennett, Prime Minister
of Canada, had a practical experience of the operation
of Governor Strong's dollar stabilisation policy, and
of the disaster which befell the United States, and
involved Canada, when that policy was abandoned
and a reversion to traditional gold standard methods
was adopted. Nevertheless, he confessed that he could
not see any alternative to gold as a currency standard.

Messrs. Bruce and Coates, representatives of Australia and New Zealand, knew by extremely bitter
experience the disasters and devastation which the
traditional gold standard had brought on all debtor
countries, and on countries producing primary
commodities. They had withdrawn from the gold
standard months before Britain withdrew, and had
therefore a longer experience of the great stimulus
towards a return to prosperity created by freedom
from the gold standard.

Mr. Havenga, representing South Africa, the
country which produced over 60 per cent of the world's

annual output of gold, naturally viewed the situation from a distinctive angle. He favoured the restoration of the gold standard, but thought that the forth-coming World Economic Conference, representing the nations of the world, would be a better instrument for such restoration than a conference of British Empire nations only.

India was represented by Sir Henry Strakosch, by far the ablest currency expert on the Committee. He was a supporter of a gold standard, but not of the traditional pre-war gold standard. He preferred the gold standard as recommended by the Genoa Conference of 1922; that is, a gold standard that would pay as much attention to the stability of prices as to the stability of the international exchanges.

Presiding over this strong Committee was Mr. Neville Chamberlain, Chancellor of the Exchequer. Possessing all the Chamberlain ability and shrewd-ness, he had sharpened them by an arduous business life. With no pretensions to be a currency expert, he explained his currency creed to the House of Commons in the following terms:

If he might express his personal opinion, he was not attracted by the idea of a managed currency. He thought that, sooner or later, they would find that they had got to link their sterling up again to a metallic basis. As to what that basis should be, whether they should stick to gold, or whether they should try to mix up with something to help gold out, he was not going to be dogmatic, although he must confess that he did not see any better basis than the gold which had in the past served them well.

Though these were his personal opinions, he informed the Committee at Ottawa that Britain had no intention of returning to a gold standard unless reassured that there would be no possibility of a breakdown similar to that which had occurred in the previous year. He stressed the fundamental world changes, economic, political and monetary, that would have to be accomplished before Britain returned to gold.

The factor that contributed most of all to the success of the Ottawa Conference from a currency point of view was the fact that its Monetary and Finance Committee was not a committee of bankers. The Cunliffe and the Bradbury Committees had been in essence committees of bankers. They viewed national interests from the windows of the bank parlour. From their point of view, industry, commerce, agriculture, wages, employment, were but counters in the skilled game of international finance. They must be regulated to fit in with the monetary scheme. The monetary scheme must not be regulated to fit in with the needs and necessities of the world. The post-war world must be thrust back into the nineteenth century, rather than the monetary system of the nineteenth century be adapted to the post-war world. The Ottawa Conference was free from such deadening influences. The members of its Monetary and Finance Committee were all closely in touch with the realities and problems of commerce and industry in the new world which had emerged from the war.

The members of the Committee had a feeling that

they were an advance committee of the World Economic Conference. This was a great advantage. It gave them the opportunity to shelve the thorny question of the return to a gold standard, and leave it to be subsequently determined by the World Economic Conference due to be held in London shortly. This was accomplished in the passage:

> While certain of the States here represented hold very definite views on the question of the most desirable standard, the Conference refrains from making any recommendation on the subject, in view of the fact that the question is shortly to be discussed at an international conference.

Underneath that sentence lies concealed the impossibility of reconciling the conflicting views of Canada and South Africa on the one hand, supporting a return to the gold standard, and Australia and New Zealand on the other, opposed to such a step.

Having satisfactorily evaded the problem of a return to gold, the Committee found that the remaining problems to be faced were thereby greatly simplified. Its report is reproduced as Appendix I to this volume. It will be observed that the term gold standard is used once only in the report, in connection with the necessity for adjusting the factors which caused the breakdown of the gold standard in many countries.

The elimination of the question of the return to gold brought the Committee at once into a position of complete agreement. The policy of the Macmillan Report—that a very large increase in the world's wholesale price level was imperatively necessary—

received unanimous and enthusiastic approval from every member of the Committee. A rise in prices is mentioned four times in Mr. Neville Chamberlain's statement, incorporated in the report. It occurs repeatedly in the report itself in such phrases as:

a rise throughout the world in the general levels of wholesale prices is in the highest degree desirable—para. 1 (*a*).
measures for raising wholesale prices—para. 1 (*b*).
help towards raising prices—para. 1 (*c*).
action towards a rise in prices—para. 1 (*d*).
a rise in the general level of wholesale prices—para. 1 (*e*).
a rise in the general level of commodity prices—para. 2.

That was the supreme and immediate currency objective—a rise in the general level of commodity prices. The return to gold was, in comparison, a negligible issue. It could be shelved, postponed, and left to the tender mercies of a World Economic Conference. It could await the adjustment of factors, political, economic, financial and monetary, which had already caused its breakdown. But a rise in the commodity price level, in the opinion of the members of the Ottawa Conference, outweighed all other currency issues, including that of the gold standard.

Though remunerative prices were the immediate objective, the permanent and ultimate objective was the stability of the price level. The equilibrium point at which stabilisation should be effected is stated in general terms as being:

a height more in keeping with the level of costs, including the burden of debts and other fixed and semi-fixed charges.

Stabilisation was to be achieved by:

international co-operation to be secured and maintained, with a view to avoiding, as far as may be found practicable, wide fluctuations in the purchasing power of standards of value.

The monetary means to accomplish the raising of prices were to be:

low rates of interest and an abundance of short-term money . . . the rate of interest for all purposes should be kept as low as financial conditions permit.

Whether the members of the Conference realised it or not, this monetary policy meant a prolonged and indefinite postponement of any possibility of the return to a gold standard. The United States and France were still accumulating vast reserves of gold. The people on the Continent were hoarding gold as rapidly as when they compelled Britain to withdraw from the gold standard. In order to preserve stocks of gold at a fixed price, the Bank of England would have had to impose a bank rate at a level far higher than that contemplated by the policy prescribed at Ottawa.

The monetary action prescribed by the Conference meant, in substance, the abandonment of the gold standard. As suggested by the quotation from *The Times* at the head of this chapter, a revival of industry required, not only low rates of interest, but a re-assurance to—

the many industrialists and others who have feared that attempts would be made to persuade Great Britain to return to the gold standard in circumstances which would make such return disastrous.

Low rates of interest meant that the Bank of England must be restricted to its legitimate sphere of currency management. It must be precluded from making disturbing and devastating intrusions into industrial management, commercial management, wage management, profit management, employment management, sales management—all the disastrous interventions into the industrial and commercial prosperity of the country specified in such detail in the Cunliffe Report of 1918. Moreover, its currency management must be restricted to an objective, that of providing exactly the amount of currency and credit required to provide the maximum of prosperity and the maximum of employment in the country.

The monetary action prescribed by the Ottawa Conference implied that the internal welfare and prosperity of the country must not be made subsidiary to the international position, as explained by Mr. Montagu Norman to the Macmillan Commission. His damaging admissions that—

especially over the last few years, so far as the international position is concerned, we have been continuously under the harrow;

and:

The main consideration in connection with the movements of the bank rate is the international consideration.

Also:

We are subject to whatever conditions may dominate the international position;

164

were sufficient to prevent him from ever again being given authority to place British industry under the harrow. Interest rates must be kept low. That meant no return to a gold standard. Whatever other methods might be necessary to stabilise the international exchanges, the damaging and primitive method of raising the bank rate must be abandoned. The gold reserves necessary for the operations of the Bank of England must be obtained by paying the market price of gold, not by penalising every branch of British industry and commerce by punitive rates of interest. The rate of interest must be at the service of the industry of the country, not at the service of an obsolete system of currency.

From one aspect, the prescription of low rates of interest may be regarded as the most revolutionary feature of the Ottawa currency policy. In Chapter II reference was made to the criticisms levelled against the encroachment by the bankers on the prerogative of Government by the creation of bank money. Such criticisms imply that the responsibility of providing all the currency needed by industry and commerce should rest on Government, and that Government should provide such a supply of currency free of all interest. For Government to rely on the banking system to provide nine-tenths of the currency required for the normal pursuits of industry and commerce, and furthermore to permit the charge of a high rate of interest, sometimes punitive rates, for such provision, is regarded by many as an abdication by Government of one of its primary responsibilities.

But at Ottawa the Governments of the British Commonwealth took one step, though not a very pronounced step, towards resuming their full prerogative over the creation of money. Bankers may still continue to create bank money, and may still continue to charge interest for it, but they are no longer free to charge whatever interest suits the convenience of the banking system. Interest for the future for all purposes must be "kept as low as financial conditions permit."

The future prosperity of the world is inseparably bound up with low rates of interest. As Mr. Keynes states:

> Hitherto the rate of interest has been too high to allow us to have all the capital goods, particularly houses, which would be useful to us.

The Cunliffe Report of 1918, in effect, says the same thing. It states that the raising of the bank rate postpones new enterprises and lessens the demand for constructional materials. The Ottawa Monetary Report is a warning that, though Government will permit the banking system to continue to create bank money, it must provide it in adequate quantities, and at low rates of interest. Never again must it be deliberately manipulated to force upon the country the appalling sequence of disasters enumerated in the Cunliffe Report.

A contemporary illustration may be given to demonstrate how inconsistent the Ottawa monetary policy of low rates of interest would be with the restoration and maintenance of the gold standard. On January 5, 1934, on the issue of a French Government loan of ten billion francs, it was officially stated that thirty billions of francs were being hoarded in France in the form of gold, bank notes and bank deposits. On October 19, 1934, on the issue of a French Government $4\frac{1}{2}$ per cent loan, it was stated that hoarding amounted to forty billions of francs. Thus, in nine and a half months French hoarding (quite apart from any additions to the Central Bank reserves) amounted to ten billions of francs, or roughly £130,000,000. This is the hoarding in France alone. Hoarding on the rest of the continent of Europe is progressing at a similar pace. It is impossible to imagine that, if Britain had been on a gold standard, and compelled to sell gold at a fixed price, the bank rate could have remained at 2 per cent in the face of the drain of gold that hoarding on such a scale would have entailed. The insistence on low rates of interest therefore precludes a return to any gold standard that can be conceived at present.

Although the members of the Ottawa Conference imagined that they had shelved the question of the return to a gold standard, they did not intend to shelve the associated problem of the stability of the international exchanges. It had hitherto been assumed that the stability of the international exchanges could be secured only by a gold standard. But the Ottawa Conference put forward the revolutionary view that a gold standard is not necessary to stabilise the international exchanges. That objective can be achieved by a common price policy of the various nations. The most creative passage in the Report reads:

> The Conference recognises the value of the countries within the Commonwealth, whose currencies are linked to sterling, maintaining stability between their exchange rates, and looks to a rise in the general level of wholesale prices as the most desirable means for facilitating this result.

This is one of the most revolutionary currency propositions ever formulated. It affirms that "the most desirable means for facilitating" "stability between their exchange rates" is not gold, not the gold standard, but the common policy of the countries working for "a rise in the general level of wholesale prices." It goes far beyond the Genoa policy—that the stability of prices should be an objective of currency management, as well as stability of the international exchanges. It places stability of prices as the primary objective. It goes farther even than that. It makes stability of the international exchanges depend on the common policy of stability of prices. Price stability is not only to be the primary objective; it is also to be the instrument to secure the secondary objective of international exchange stability.

The members of the Ottawa Conference "builded better than they knew." In the second section of their Report they thought they had shelved consideration of the gold standard. They quite overlooked the fact that in the first section they had twice gone far towards repudiating it. They had prescribed low interest rates which are inconsistent with the maintenance of a gold standard. They had dismissed gold as being the most natural means for regulating the international exchanges, by using the superlative phrase "most desirable means" with respect to an alternative method which was henceforth to be adopted.

Although this revolutionary method of stabilising the international exchanges was to be initiated between the "countries within the Commonwealth," it was not to be confined to them. The Conference

considered the possibility of achieving valuable results by creating an area of stability among countries regulating their currencies in relation to sterling;—

and also recognised

the great importance to traders of stability of exchange rates over as wide an area as possible.

Here is a complete and logical proposal for an international currency system independent of gold, which would secure the stabilisation of both prices and the international exchanges. The nations of the British Commonwealth, and the countries regulating their currencies in relation to sterling, should first work together for a considerable rise in world wholesale prices. This common price policy will, in itself, tend to stabilise the international exchanges between such nations and countries. In due course world wholesale prices will reach a level at which they can be stabilised. Such stabilisation, if effected in co-operation with the countries so acting together, will further contribute to the stability of the international exchanges. This currency system is not confined to the British Empire, but to all countries willing to associate their currencies with sterling.

The Ottawa Report is in no doubt whatever as to which should take precedence, the raising and stabilisation of prices or the stabilisation of the international exchanges. The latter

must await the restoration of conditions for the satisfactory working of an international standard, as referred to below.

That is, they must await

a rise in the general level of commodity prices in various countries to a height more in keeping with the level of costs, including the burden of debts and other fixed and semi-fixed charges;

and also await

an adjustment of factors, political, economic, financial and monetary, which have caused the breakdown of the gold standard in many countries, and which, if not adjusted, would inevitably lead to another breakdown of whatever international standard may be adopted.

The members of the Ottawa Conference took full advantage of the freedom conferred by leaving the consideration of the gold standard to the subsequent determination of the World Economic Conference. It enabled them to conduct their deliberations without any reference to the question whether their proposals were consistent with the restoration of the gold standard or not. It permitted them to formulate two lines of policy:

low rates of interest,
stabilisation of the international exchanges by the method of common price policies,

neither of which were consistent with the gold standard. It also enabled them to refer to the future international currency standard in terms which made no suggestion or implication that a return to gold was considered either advisable or necessary. Such references are as follows:

An international standard as referred to below;
The ultimate aim of monetary policy should be the restoration of a satisfactory international monetary standard;
There are, however, several conditions precedent to the re-establishment of any international monetary standard;
Whatever international standard may be adopted;
The future working of any international standard.

They avoid the mention of a gold standard and indicate complete independence of a return to the gold standard.

The Ottawa Monetary Report mentions as a condition precedent to the re-establishment of any international monetary standard the adjustment of factors, political, economic, financial and monetary, which have caused the breakdown of the gold standard in many countries. These four factors may be briefly summarised:

Political.—The gold standard is essentially a "Free Trade" system of currency, implying the settlement of the international balance of trade, as far as possible, in goods; and, to as small an extent as possible, by movements of gold. It is an impossible system in a world of high Protective Tariffs, Quotas, Exchange Restrictions, and other hindrances to the utmost freedom of international commerce.

Economic.—The gold standard can only obtain its objective of stabilisation of the exchanges by disastrous interventions, causing extreme depression of industry and commerce, as specified in the Cunliffe Report of 1918. Such methods are ruled out for the future.

Financial.—The gold standard needs an equitable distribution of gold throughout all the countries of the world in order that every country may be able to finance its legitimate requirements without being compelled to sell its produce at a loss on a falling market. There is no such equitable distribution at present.

Monetary.—The gold standard depends on an annual increase of monetary gold, proportionate to the annual rate of increase of the world's commerce and industry. The abstraction of immense quantities of gold for hoarding purposes renders it unable to fulfil its currency functions.

These were the four principal factors which caused the breakdown of the gold standard.

The members of the Ottawa Conference may have imagined that they were merely creating a provisional currency to carry on until the World Economic Conference should be in a position to consider the restoration of the gold standard. But they achieved much more than this. They formulated an international currency system capable of working permanently on lines completely independent of the gold standard. Instead of merely shelving the gold standard, they had supplied an alternative. By omitting all reference to the possibility of a return to the gold standard, they created the impression that an international currency system independent of gold was feasible, and gave such a system an opportunity of demonstrating its feasibility in practice.

The revolutionary nature of the Ottawa proposals were not at first appreciated. The Ottawa Monetary Report was quite overshadowed by the tariff activities of the Conference. When it was issued, *The Times* denied it a position on its central page, relegated it, mostly in small print, to a subsidiary page, and made the comment:

As has been anticipated, it does not suggest any spectacular methods for dealing with the position.

After five days' consideration, however, *The Times* changed its view as to its importance, and admitted that:

the Report is far more valuable and important than may have appeared on a casual reading.

It then made the comments reproduced as the introduction to this chapter.

Despite the fact that it was overshadowed by the impending World Economic Conference, the international currency system inaugurated at Ottawa proved a success. It filled a much-needed want. It banded together the nations of the British Commonwealth in a concerted effort to secure remunerative prices for their produce, and to restore stability to sterling. It gave official recognition to the currency federation sometimes known as Sterlingaria, the countries regulating their currencies in relation to sterling.

It provided a definite basis for the operation of the Exchange Equalisation Fund. Quite apart from the ultimate stability of sterling which was its final objective it gave a measure of immediate stability to sterling by linking it to a determinate currency programme. It dispelled the nightmare of the industrialists that an immediate return to the gold standard was contemplated. The countries associated with sterling found confidence both in the methods and the final objectives of the programme outlined. The countries producing primary commodities regained hope at the initiation of a new currency system backed by the resources of the British Empire, and designed to secure, as its first objective, a substantial rise in the prices of their produce. Sterling was no longer a passive supine currency, at the mercy of every cross-current of exchange speculation. It was definitely brought under the control of forces moving inevitably towards complete stabilisation.

Besides achieving an unexpected practical success, the Ottawa policy had one result which no one had anticipated. The most serious challenger to gold as a standard of currency was not silver, but the wholesale price index. It had established a footing in the United States during Governor Strong's dollar stabilisation policy. But it had been discredited by the collapse of 1929, and had not since been revived. But the success of the Ottawa policy in raising the wholesale price level could only be measured by a price index. That revolutionary term had not even been mentioned in the Ottawa Monetary Report. Nevertheless, it was the only standard by which the Ottawa policy could be measured or judged; and, consequently, the only serious competitor with gold as the future currency standard was brought into the heart of the new currency system.

Gold was challenged by the Ottawa Monetary Report on three counts; as being a wasteful and disturbing regulator of the international rates of exchange; as being an obstacle to the low rates of interest essential for industrial prosperity; and, as being an inefficient and fluctuating standard of value. In all three directions the Ottawa policy promised a marked improvement. It had twelve months in which to establish itself before it had to face the great crucial test, a critical investigation by the World Economic Conference. Its future depended on the manner in which it adapted itself to the requirements of the world during that period.

Meantime, the advocates for return to the gold standard were busy. Mention has been made in Chapter IV of the review of the Ottawa policy by Professor Robbins. He commenced by depreciating the Ottawa Monetary Report as being of no importance, stating that—

it would be an exaggeration to claim great importance for the result of the deliberations on monetary policy. . . . The most that could be hoped was that positive commitments could be avoided, and agreement secured on the negative issues of what policies to avoid. This indeed seems to have been the outcome.

He gradually works up to his objective—a more severe and repressive administration of the gold standard than that which put Britain under the harrow in the years 1925–31—expressed in the passage:

> If we are to avoid inflationary disturbances, the authorities in the financial centres must work the gold standard on lines much more severe than those which have been the rule in recent years.

He anticipates an easy victory for the gold standard over such an inane and feeble competitor at the World Economic Conference, celebrating its triumph in advance in the passage:

> The document which has been issued embodying the conclusions of the Committee on Money and Finance is a vague pronouncement which, while it may justify the claim that deliberations have taken place, in fact commits no one to anything which may be inconvenient in the more practical negotiations of the forthcoming World Economic Conference.

Professor Robbins thus proved himself to be completely out of touch with the post-war world of currency and finance. His essay in prophecy was as lamentable a failure as those of Lord Bradbury and the late Mr. Goodenough. How "this vague pronouncement" which "commits no one to anything," this document which avoided "positive commitments" and secured agreement on "negative issues," which was not even going to be inconvenient, shattered the World Economic Conference, must be recorded in a future chapter.

CHAPTER X

THE EXCHANGE EQUALISATION
FUND

"The Conference has noted with satisfaction that the United Kingdom has already established machinery aiming at preventing wide fluctuations in gold value of sterling by speculative movements."—The Ottawa Monetary Report.

WITHOUT actually mentioning the Exchange Equalisation Fund, the Ottawa Conference noted its establishment with satisfaction, and regarded it as an essential factor in carrying out its policy of stabilising international exchange rates. The Exchange Equalisation Fund had been strongly recommended by the Macmillan Report in the passages:

The magnitude of London's international operations to-day requires that the normal level of the Bank of England's liquid international assets should be materially higher than it now is, that these liquid assets should exist to be used at frequent intervals, and that the money markets at home and abroad should be made accustomed to view these operations as a sign of strength and as part of the Bank's regular machinery for the control of credit. We consider that, at present, the disparity between London's liquid resources and those of other large international countries is too great and should be diminished.

And:

We suggest that in addition to gold reserves fluctuating between (say) £100,000,000 and £175,000,000, the Bank might maintain other foreign and liquid resources fluctuating in amount up to £50,000,000.

This was a recommendation to increase the Bank of England's reserves by £50 millions. That recommendation was made when Britain was still on the gold standard. But, when Britain withdrew from the gold standard, a problem as to the future international currency immediately arose. Britain had been regarded by the world as the natural provider of an international currency since the institution of the gold standard in 1816. What would happen now that Britain had withdrawn from the gold standard? Neither France nor the United States had the inclination or the machinery with which to operate an international currency on their own initiative. They were much more concerned with the national, rather than the international, aspects and operations of currency.

There were only two alternatives. Either international currency must be allowed to drift without guidance or control, or Britain must undertake the responsibility of re-establishing it on a new basis, now that gold had largely forsaken currency functions in order to supply the revived demand for hoarding. There was no difficulty in providing Britain itself with a purely inconvertible national paper currency.

But had Britain the capacity to supply the world with an international paper currency? Most of the rest of the world had a strong metallic complex in currency matters. Their national currencies were nearly all on a metallic basis. Could an international paper currency, sponsored by Britain, secure their confidence?

Experience suggested that Britain possessed this capacity. During the latter half of the nineteenth century most of the international commerce of the world had been transacted by means of a paper currency, the Sterling Bills of Exchange. True, there was a gold reserve in the background. But, thanks to Free Trade, and to the excellent organisation of the London Money Market, gold had remained in the background. The active functions of an international currency for over half a century had been effected by paper money, with international gold movements as an almost negligible factor.

Moreover, during the period 1919 to 1925, although the pound sterling had been but a unit of inconvertible paper currency, it had held its own in the international field, with the dollar, which was on a gold basis. Also, after September 1931, although there was a momentary distrust of the paper pound, as soon as it had fallen to its natural value it speedily resumed a pre-eminent place in international commerce as a universally accepted currency.

Experience therefore demonstrated that the position which the pound sterling had established as an international currency was due to the wisdom of its management and control, and to the efficiency with which it performed its currency functions through the agency of the London Money Market, and not to any association it may have had in the past with gold. As there was no immediate prospect of a return to a gold standard, it was decided that every endeavour must be made to enable sterling to act as an international currency, even though it was inconvertible and not associated with gold. The steps taken towards this end at Ottawa have been recorded in the previous chapter.

The establishment of the Exchange Equalisation Fund was complementary to the Ottawa policy in maintaining the international position of the pound sterling on a paper basis. Britain's control of the gold standard had often been in jeopardy owing to the inadequacy of the gold reserve of the Bank of England. Despite Mr. Montagu Norman's thrice-repeated "It is effective" (see Chapter III), the Macmillan Report recommended that the Bank of England Reserve should be increased by £50 millions.

But the maintenance of an international currency on a paper basis required a much stronger reserve than the maintenance of an international gold standard. It was a much more severe task in a world saturated with a reverence for gold and distrust of paper. To many it appeared a task beyond the realms of possibility. Still it was being attempted; and that being the case, it was essential that it should be backed by adequate reserves.

The normal reserves of the Bank of England have, since the war, fluctuated round about £150 millions. Instead of strengthening them by £50 millions, as recommended by the Macmillan Report, they were doubled by the addition of an Exchange Equalisation Fund of £150 millions. This was found to be inadequate, and the Exchange Equalisation Fund was subsequently raised to £350 millions, making the total Bank Reserves £500 millions. Of these £500 millions, about £150 millions are held in gold, and the rest, known as the Exchange Equalisation Fund, in sterling paper or foreign exchange.

Compared with the gold reserves of France and the United States, each approximating £1,000 millions, the reserves of Britain, now expanded to half that amount, but with only £150 millions held in gold, may seem utterly inadequate. The disparity is enhanced when the heavy international responsibilities of Britain are compared with those of France and the United States. But there is a fundamental difference between the principles on which these reserves of gold operate. The high reserves of France and the United States are necessitated by the demand of the citizens of those countries for convertibility. The United States has abandoned convertibility for the time being. But slightly to paraphrase Mr. Cross's query, and applying it to the United States (see Appendix IV)—

if there was no probability of their ever going back on the gold standard, and if they knew there was no chance of their doing that, and that they would always have an inconvertible paper, it would have a terrific effect on them.

The gold reserves of the United States and France are kept, in fact, much more as a backing for their internal currencies than as a basis for international currency.

The exact contrary is the case in Britain. Its internal currency does not require the backing of a single ounce of gold. The Macmillan Report correctly explains the nature of the Bank of England Reserve in the passage:

> Formerly, when the Bank's gold was held for two purposes, partly to meet an external drain and partly to meet an internal drain, it may have been reasonable to earmark a substantial part of it for the latter purpose. But now that the second purpose has disappeared, and has, in fact, been abolished by law, the gold reserve of the Bank of England is held for no other purpose than to meet a foreign drain.

The reserve of approximately £500 millions of the Bank of England is therefore available in its entirety as a basis for international currency. About £150 millions are kept in gold, and £350 millions are used as an International Currency Management Fund. The methods and objectives of this Fund are exhaustively and authoritatively explained in Appendix IV to this volume. It comprises an extract from the evidence given by Dr. Sprague to the Sub-Committee of the House of Representatives on Banking and Currency on February 22, 1934. No full account of the working of this Fund has hitherto been published in Britain. Dr. Sprague was Financial Adviser to the Bank of England when the Fund was established, and continued in that appointment for the first year of its operations, so no better exposition of its working could possibly be given.

Reference has already been made (Chapter VI) to Dr. Sprague's insistence on the fact that the operation of the Exchange Equalisation Fund tended to keep the pound sterling at its neutral value. It was not an active motive force, but a stabilising force, smoothing out fluctuations, steadying oscillations, acting rather as a governor than as a brake or stimulant. But, with the initiation of the Ottawa policy, the pound sterling was not allowed to remain at a neutral value. Instead of being passive and remaining neutral, it became an active factor in securing a rise in the wholesale price level. A neutral pound meant that the value of the pound sterling was governed by the world price level, as explained in Chapter VI. The Ottawa policy meant just the opposite, that, as far as possible, the world price level must be governed by the pound sterling.

The Ottawa Monetary Report had specified low rates of interest as the principal monetary factor which could contribute towards a rise in the wholesale price level. But a Currency Management Fund of £350 millions is a potent monetary factor, not only in smoothing out fluctuations, but also in assisting in securing more positive objectives, such as a rise in world wholesale prices. The Ottawa policy was an ambitious and arduous policy. It found a world of pessimism, a world without confidence, a world suffering from a protracted fall of prices. It proposed to transform it into a world of optimism, a world of confidence, a world of rising prices. It was a desperate and an uphill task. But with a fund of £350 millions at its back to smooth the way, to even out the ups and downs on the path, and to contribute a constant and steady pull in the right direction, its chances of success were greatly increased.

The Exchange Equalisation Fund assisted the
Ottawa policy in another manner. Under the Ottawa
policy the stabilisation of the international exchange
rates was to be effected through a common price policy
of the participating nations. But this would necessarily
be a very slow process. It was an experimental and
unfamiliar method, with no tradition or experience
behind it, and with no prescribed rules or technique
for its guidance. Without being able to do more than
smooth out the worst fluctuations of the exchanges,
the Exchange Equalisation Fund assisted greatly in
the initial steps of the Ottawa Currency System in
tending to produce the stability of international
exchange rates by means of the common price policy
of these nations associating their currencies with
sterling.

Any reader who may wish to get an insight into the
inner workings of the Exchange Equalisation Fund
may do so by a study of Appendix IV. It is rather with
respect to its external reactions that it is relevant to
the Currency Revolution in progress when it was
initiated. It marks a distinct departure from the gold
standard system of international currency. It gives the
Bank of England a far greater reserve than would be
necessary under the gold standard system. It intro-
duces new, and ultimately much more efficient,
methods of stabilising the international exchanges. It
enables rates of interest to be governed with sole
regard for the needs of industry. It avoids the disastrous
and artificial sequence of disorders specified in the

Cunliffe Report of 1918. It is an active factor in co-operating with the Ottawa system of currency in securing the three great objectives of an international currency, remunerative prices, stable prices and stable international rates of exchange.

Though the Exchange Equalisation Fund implies a more or less permanent departure from a gold standard, it does not imply that gold will necessarily be divested of all its monetary functions. It enables a more efficient distribution of monetary functions to be effected, somewhat on the following lines:

A store of savings;—gold.
International currency:

   (a) settlements within the Balance of Trade;—paper currency, such as bills of exchange;
   (b) settlements outside the Balance of Trade;—gold, but at market price, not at a fixed price.

Internal currency:

   (a) large transactions, amounting to nine-tenths of the internal transactions of a country;—paper currency, cheques;
   (b) small transactions, such as wages, travelling expenses and pocket money;—bank notes, silver token money.

Internal Reserves, where the people demand a high standard of convertibility;—gold.

International Reserves:

   (a) for the normal working of a paper international currency system;—sterling paper and foreign exchange, the Exchange Equalisation Fund.
   (b) for special emergencies;—gold.

The Internal Standard of Value;—a managed standard, based on an equilibrium point on a Cost of Living Index.

The International Standard of Value;—a managed standard, based on an equilibrium point on an accepted wholesale Price Index.

At the present moment the Exchange Equalisation Fund is performing four functions. Its primary function is that of smoothing out exchange fluctuations. In addition, it is assisting materially in raising the world wholesale price level. It is also keeping sterling in touch with the dollar on the one hand, and the franc on the other. The two last-mentioned functions are by no means simple. The spasmodic changes in the gold content of the dollar, and even the apprehension of such changes, cause wide and rapid fluctuations of the foreign exchanges which tax the whole resources of the Exchange Equalisation Fund before equilibrium can be restored.

But the necessity of keeping in touch with the franc is of much more importance than that of keeping in touch with the dollar. It is becoming increasingly apparent that the countries on the gold bloc cannot maintain much longer their attitude of aloofness from the currency developments of the modern world. It is difficult to foresee for how long they will endure the declining exports resulting from their adherence to an obsolete form of the gold standard; or what their line of retreat will be when they eventually take the inevitable step and associate themselves with the rest of the world in the evolution of a rational system of currency. Whenever the step is taken, it will have grave repercussions on the stability of all currencies, more especially on sterling. The closer the Exchange Equalisation Fund enables the franc to keep in touch with sterling, the easier will be the transition when it comes.

The position of the countries on the gold bloc is the most difficult currency problem of the day. While all other countries are beginning to experience a feeling of revival, the depression in Western Europe grows deeper. It will need the helpful and sympathetic co-operation of all nations to ease the difficulties of the transition for them when it comes. The most valuable factor in minimising its disturbing effects will be the British Exchange Equalisation Fund.

CHAPTER XI

THE BRITISH EMPIRE CURRENCY DECLARATION

"While certain of the States here represented hold very definite views on the question of the most desirable standard, the Ottawa Conference refrains from making any recommendation on the subject, in view of the fact that the question is shortly to be discussed at an international conference."—
The Ottawa Monetary Report.

THERE are five candidates for the honour of having killed the World Economic Conference:

> President Roosevelt,
> The French Delegation, under M. Daladier,
> The City of London, organised by Mr. Montagu Norman,
> *The Times*,
> The Ottawa Currency System.

The initial preparations for the Conference were made in Paris. It became very clear during the course of these preliminaries that the French delegates would demand the restoration of the gold standard as an international currency system at the Conference, and would not be prepared to participate unless such restoration were given a prominent position on the Agenda. This was confirmed by M. Deladier, the Head of the French Delegation, who, in the opening stages of the Conference, made the following statement as to the French position:—

The economic problems cannot be settled unless and until currencies are stabilised and the return to the gold standard is carried out.

This was interpreted by every delegate at the Conference to mean that France would not continue to participate unless both Britain and the United States were prepared to return to the Gold Standard.

On June 26, 1933, just as the Conference opened, *The Times* issued a magnificent Special Gold Number, written round the text:—

One of the most important tasks of the World Economic Conference, which is sitting here in London, will be to prepare a way for the return to exchange stability through the rehabilitation of the gold standard.

It was issued at exactly the right moment to create the impression among the delegates from the sixty odd nations taking part in the Conference, that Britain was ready and willing to return to the Gold Standard, and was only awaiting the meeting of the Conference to declare its intention.

The financial interests of the City of London had previously been greatly perturbed by the announcement in *The Times*, after the Ottawa Report had been issued, that:

it (the Ottawa Report) should assure the many industrialists and others who have feared that attempts would be made to persuade Britain to return to the gold standard in circumstances which would make such a return disastrous.

The Ottawa Monetary Report may have reassured the industrialists. It certainly did not reassure the financial interests of the City of London. Their opposition was stimulated by carefully arranged propaganda. With the assistance of the representatives of the Central Banks in attendance at the World Economic Conference, a carefully worked out set of exchange parities was prepared. These were embodied in a proposal, emanating from the Central Banks, that a temporary stabilisation of the exchanges between the pound, the dollar and the franc should be effected.

President Roosevelt had withdrawn the United States from the gold standard shortly before the Conference, partly because he saw that the French policy was designed to force his hand, and partly because he wished to be perfectly free from international currency entanglements in his efforts to extricate the United States from the worst financial crisis in the course of its history. When the proposal of the Central Banks was brought to his notice, he gave a firm but very courteous negative to the proposal that the United States should participate in any such stabilisation of the international exchanges.

Throughout these preliminary manœuvres the British Empire delegates were silent. The Ottawa currency policy had succeeded beyond their expectations. They had prepared a statement to bring to the notice of the Conference the progress made towards the realisation of the objectives they had suggested for the nations of the British Commonwealth and for the countries associated with the sterling to pursue. But in the welter of intrigue they never found an opportunity of presenting it. They had intentionally refrained at Ottawa from making any recommendations concerning the most desirable international currency standard that the world should adopt, considering that this issue would be discussed at the World Economic Conference.

But they found that there was to be no discussion. The issue had been settled in advance of the meeting of the Conference by the French Delegation, *The Times*, and the City of London, assisted by the representatives of the Central Banks then in London. All that the Conference had to do was officially to confirm the return to a gold standard which had already been decided on its behalf. The British Empire Delegation was flouted. The actively working official international currency system of the nations of the British Commonwealth was dismissed as if it were non-existent. The policy of stabilising international exchanges by the method of common price policies was airily put aside. The fact that at an Imperial Conference it had been officially proclaimed as the most desirable means for facilitating the maintenance of stability between exchange rates was treated with contempt. The measures taken at Ottawa for—

achieving valuable results by creating an area of stability among countries regulating their currencies in relation to sterling—

were ignored, despite the fact that they actually had achieved valuable results, and actually had succeeded in creating an area of stability among the countries allied to sterling.

Such a practical matter as the inauguration of a new and successfully working system of international currency was of too trivial a nature to obtain the attention of the Conference. The members of the triple alliance for the rehabilitation of the gold standard had determined that another attempt should be made to obtain the participation of President Roosevelt in their manœuvres. A second and more cautiously worded proposal for a temporary international exchange stabilisation was made, this time direct from the Conference. But they had mistaken their man. This time he made his famous reply of July 3, 1933, in such vigorous language that, according to popular opinion, it killed the Conference.

In the extremely critical times of the early days of his tenure of office, President Roosevelt received valuable backing from the Committee for the Nation, a Committee of two thousand leaders of American industry and agriculture. It has steadily and consistently advocated Reflation, and the Stabilisation of Prices at a remunerative level. The British Empire Delegates at the World Economic Conference owe a debt of gratitude to this Committee for its unwavering support of President Roosevelt when he routed the forces massed against the Ottawa Currency Policy.

As a matter of fact nobody can be saddled with the responsibility of having killed the World Economic

Conference. It never lived. It was stillborn. The atmosphere of intrigue in which it was brought to birth was too stifling for it to take a living breath. As a Conference, aiming to find a solution of the world's difficulties, it never existed. As an Economic Conference, the world was not ready for it. As a Monetary Conference, it had been rendered superfluous by the success of the Ottawa currency system.

Whether by accident or design, President Roosevelt's reply of July 3rd was the statement, in most vigorous language, of a policy identical with that of the Ottawa Monetary Report. His reply is reproduced as Appendix III to this volume, and it is interesting to compare the Ottawa policy as described in Appendix I, with President Roosevelt's policy as outlined in Appendix III. The raising of prices of the Ottawa policy is "the dollar value we hope to attain in the near future" of President Roosevelt. "The avoidance of wide fluctuations in the purchasing power of standards of value" in the Ottawa Report, is President Roosevelt's "dollar which a generation hence will have the same purchasing and debt-paying power as the dollar value we hope to attain in the near future." President Roosevelt's "old fetishes of so-called international bankers" and his "basic economic errors that underlie so much of the present world-wide depression" are among the "factors, political, economic, financial and monetary, which have caused the breakdown of the gold standard in many countries" mentioned in the Ottawa Report. President Roosevelt's "sound internal economic system of a nation" is the Ottawa system of low rates of interest, abundance of short-term money, and the rate of interest for all purposes kept as low as financial conditions permit. The common price policies of the Ottawa Report are President Roosevelt's "efforts to plan national currencies with the objective of giving to those currencies a continuing purchasing power which does not vary in terms of commodities and needs of civilisation." The Ottawa Policy of the stabilisation of international exchange rates by means of a common price policy is President Roosevelt's "broad purpose, the stabilisation of every nation's currency."

Another interesting method of comparing the policy of President Roosevelt's reply with the Ottawa currency system is to compare both of them, as given in Appendices I and III, with the following abstract of the reply of President Roosevelt from *The Times* Editorial on "Two Visions of Stability" in its issue of July 4, 1933:

Mr. Roosevelt takes an exactly opposite view. Let each country, he says, take the measures necessary to put its economic system on a sound basis, and then, when prices have been raised to the required level, let it keep its currency stable in terms of goods and services. When that is done, so he appears to argue, the different currencies will naturally be stable in terms of one another. He maintains that it is this natural stability which the Conference should seek, and he strongly resents attempts to distract it from this object by the proposal of a purely artificial and temporary experiment, affecting the monetary exchange of a few nations only.

That is an excellent summary of President Roosevelt's policy. It is also an excellent summary of the Ottawa Monetary Report. To paraphrase Euclid's principle that things which are equal to the same thing are equal to one another, it may fairly be assumed that two policies which can be summarised in identical terms are identical policies. The Ottawa policy has three stages:

i. The raising of wholesale prices to a remunerative level.
ii. The stabilisation of prices when a remunerative level has been reached.
iii. The stabilisation of the international exchanges through the common price policies of the participating nations.

These three stages are expressed in *The Times* summary of President Roosevelt's reply in the following terms:

i. When prices have been raised to the required level,
ii. keep its currency stable in terms of goods and services,
iii. the different currencies will naturally be stable in terms of one another.

The World Economic Conference has usually been regarded as a struggle between President Roosevelt and the nations of the gold bloc. That is but a superficial aspect of the conflict. It was, in reality, a combined effort on the part of the City of London, the French Delegation and *The Times* to destroy the newly established Ottawa currency system. The Ottawa system was but an international expansion of Governor

Strong's dollar stabilisation policy. It was known that President Roosevelt was an adherent of Governor Strong's policy and the attack was made in order to destroy the Ottawa system, before it could establish itself and become associated with President Roosevelt's similar currency policy in the United States.

Desperate efforts were made to save the Conference after President Roosevelt's message had been received. In the confusion that resulted, the British Empire Delegates found no opportunity to present their report on the working of the new international currency system, which had been established at Ottawa and had achieved an unexpected measure of success in the short period of its existence. It was not till after the Conference had closed that they were able to issue a Declaration. When it was known that the Conference could no longer be embarrassed by the knowledge that the Ottawa currency system had proved a success, a hurried meeting of the British Delegation was called, and a Currency Declaration stating the results of the working of the Ottawa currency system was issued on July 27, 1933. That Declaration is reproduced as Appendix II to this volume, and may conveniently be termed the British Empire Currency Declaration.

The following passage from the tenth paragraph of the British Empire Currency Declaration, bears a striking resemblance to *The Times* summary of President Roosevelt's message previously quoted:

In the meantime the undersigned delegations recognise the importance of the stability of exchange rates between the countries of the Empire in the interests of trade. This objective will be constantly kept in mind in determining their monetary policy, and its achievement will be aided by the pursuit of a common policy of raising price levels. . . . The adherence of other countries to a policy on similar lines would make possible the attainment and maintenance of exchange stability over a still wider area.

The attainment of international exchange stability by means of a common price policy was a revolutionary currency policy which was first enunciated at Ottawa. The Genoa Conference of 1922 had approached near to it, but had not quite discovered it. In less than one year it was accepted as a commonplace, and regarded by the British Empire Currency Declaration as the most natural method of attaining stability of the exchanges between nation and nation. Stability of the international exchanges by means of the gold standard brings disaster to nations following divergent price policies. In the language of President Roosevelt's message, it is an artificial stability. It is artificial because it is secured by the artificial disorganisation of the internal commerce and industry of the countries affected, instead of by the more natural method of similar currency objectives. The only natural stability of the exchanges is that produced by identical price policies, or as *The Times* expresses it in its summary of President Roosevelt's message:

the different currencies will naturally be stable in terms of each other.

Unfortunately, the confusion in which the British Empire Currency Declaration was prepared and issued, precluded it from being revised and edited with the care that a document of such importance should have received. The following passage from paragraph 9 is an illustration of the confusion that existed:

The undersigned Delegations now reaffirm their view that the ultimate aim of monetary policy should be the restoration of a satisfactory international *gold* standard, under which international co-operation would be secured and maintained, with a view to avoiding, so far as may be found practicable, undue fluctuations in the purchasing power of gold.

This passage was evidently inserted in an attempt to placate the attacking gold forces, before President Roosevelt had routed them. A reference to Appendix I will show that the Delegates had never made such an affirmation at Ottawa. Their affirmation at Ottawa was in favour of—

the restoration of a satisfactory international *monetary* standard,

not—

the restoration of a satisfactory international *gold* standard.

The delegates reaffirmed something which they had never affirmed. At Ottawa they had deliberately refrained from recommending the restoration of a gold standard, and they had given reasons for so refraining. And yet they were reduced to such a state of confusion and fear by the massed attack upon them that they quite overlooked and misrepresented what actually had been affirmed at Ottawa. The discrepancy is interesting as evidence of the violence of the attack on the Ottawa policy and of the extreme confusion it produced.

The reaffirmation is as unmeaning as it is inaccurate. The word "ultimate" postpones any conceivable return to gold to an imaginary future. The phrase "undue fluctuations in the purchasing power of gold" is an admission of its unsuitability to provide a fixed standard of value. The phrase "as far as may be found practicable," expresses doubts whether stability of the value of gold will ever be attainable.

The British Empire Currency Declaration confirmed the Ottawa policy of raising the wholesale price level, and is much more definite than the Ottawa Monetary Report on the question of stabilisation when a remunerative price level has been attained. The Governments of the British Commonwealth, it states—

should persist by all means in their power, monetary and economic, within the limits of sound finance, in the policy of furthering the rise in wholesale prices, until there is evidence that equilibrium has been re-established, and that thereupon they should take whatever measures are possible to stabilise the position thus attained.

In its definition of the equilibrium of the price level at which currency should be stabilised, the British Empire Currency Declaration made a memorable and permanent contribution to the history of currency management. In Chapter II, attention was drawn to the difficulty of defining currency "inflation" or "deflation" because of the absence of any authoritative criterion as to what was the ideally right quantity of money. The term "reflation" has not been warmly accepted by economists, partly because they were unable to define it satisfactorily, and partly because they have been doubtful whether it meant anything that could be practically attempted or accomplished. Roughly speaking, reflation means the policy of stabilising the purchasing power of money. The sixth paragraph of the British Empire Currency Declaration goes much further than this, and states three objectives which a policy of reflation must secure. Though it does not use the term "Reflation" it gives an excellent description of the objectives by which any policy of reflation must be judged. The equilibrium level at which the stabilisation of the price level should be stabilised is thus defined:

> Any price level would be satisfactory which restores the normal activity of industry and employment, which ensures an economic return to the producer of primary commodities, and which harmonises the burden of debts and fixed charges with economic capacity.

The momentous and revolutionary nature of this statement of currency objectives can only be appreciated by comparing it with the statement of currency methods in the Cunliffe Report issued only fifteen years previously (see Chapter IV). In 1918 it was regarded as being essential for currency management to be prepared to postpone new enterprises, to lessen the demand for constructional materials and other capital goods, to slacken employment and to diminish the demand for consumable goods. In 1933 such currency methods were regarded with horror and abhorrence, and it was prescribed that the first aim of currency management should be to restore "the normal activity of industry and employment."

In 1918 it was considered that a necessary part of the "automatic" working of the gold standard should be to confront holders of stocks of commodities with the prospect of falling prices, and to force them to press their goods on a weak market. In 1933 so great a revolution had been affected that the second objective of currency management was to "secure an economic return to the producer of primary commodities."

In 1918 currency management included within its methods the deliberate confrontation of holders of stocks of commodities carried largely with borrowed money with an increase in interest charges, and with an actual difficulty in renewing loans. In 1933 this iniquitous treatment of industrial and commercial borrowers had been so modified that the third objective of currency management was defined as being to harmonise "the burden of debts and fixed charges with economic capacity."

Under cover of the pretence that the gold standard was automatic, the Bank of England, though admittedly it had no direct contact with industry, had repeatedly and systematically intervened with devastating effects in destroying the progress of British industry. The British Empire Currency Declaration, in the memorable passage just quoted, put an end for all time to this subordination of industry to the claims of finance. Finance in future must be the handmaid of industry, not its arbitrary and tyrannical oppressor.

The Ottawa currency system severely curtailed the freedom of the banking system to issue and manage bank money purely for its own convenience. It prescribed low rates of interest, and practically precluded any restriction of credit except on a national emergency. But the British Empire Currency Declaration went much further than this. It prescribed positive rules regulating the issue of bank money. It must be available in such quantities that it will restore the normal activity of industry and employment. It must be maintained in adequate volume to ensure an economic return to the producer of primary commodities. It must be managed so that it harmonises the burden of debts and fixed charges with economic capacity. These, and not the international movements of gold, are to be the prime considerations for future currency management. The international movements of gold had proved to be blind and false guides as to the regulation of British credit and currency. British industry had been sacrificed simply because a speculative mania had raged in the United States; and again because a hoarding mania raged on the continent of Europe. For the future, the Bank of England will not be able to place British industry "under the harrow" on account of such remote and irrelevant occurrences. The currency system must in future be managed for national, and not for sectional, interests. The Government in the British Empire Currency Declaration took a second step towards resuming its prerogative as the supreme currency authority of the nation.

The three objectives of the equilibrium price level, completely dispel the confusion regarding the terms "inflation" and "deflation" of currency. If the quantity of currency in circulation satisfies the three tests, and secures the three objectives, it is the duty of the currency authorities to maintain this position of equilibrium by all means in their power. If there is less than this quantity of money, there is "deflation." If there is more, there is "inflation." Reflation is the policy of actively correcting a position of inflation or deflation and of maintaining the position of equilibrium when achieved by the normal methods of currency management.

The striking identity between the currency policy actually adopted by the British Empire and the countries of the Sterling Group, and the currency policy towards which the United States is progressing, can best be appreciated by a comparison of the passage from the British Empire Currency Declaration quoted on page 200 above and the Resolution adopted by the American Farm Bureau Federation in November 1934. The latter Resolution reads:

We urge the President to make full use of the powers granted to him to raise the price of gold to the limits prescribed by Congress to the end:—

(1) that commodity prices may be raised in line with the debt level and fixed costs;

(2) that all business may be increased with resultant increase in employment and decrease in the huge expenditure for relief;

(3) that equities may be restored in farms, homes, and investments;

(4) that home and other building may be made possible.

The similarity of the British and American objectives is remarkable. Both stress the necessity of bringing debts and fixed costs into harmony with prices. Both make the raising of commodity prices the first aim of currency policy. Both emphasise the necessity of increasing employment. Both proclaim the restoration and maintenance of industrial activity as the cardinal objective of monetary administration.

But the similarity is not complete. The British statement is that of a revolution actually accomplished. It is a description of an actively working policy actually in operation. It was issued in the flush of success at the defeat of a massed attack from a powerful triple alliance. It had a successful record of eleven months to its credit. It was firmly established throughout the British Empire and the nations of the Sterling Group.

On the other hand, the Resolutions of the American Organisations are stages in a revolution not yet completely effected. They show the powers at the disposal of President Roosevelt not yet fully put into operation. The support of the Agricultural and Farm Organisations given to Governor Strong in his dollar stabilisation policy has already been mentioned in Chapter V above. In the meantime, Britain has not only wholeheartedly adopted that policy and trans-

formed it into an international currency system, but
has made it the basis of industrial recovery throughout
a large portion of the world. The Resolutions of the
Farm Organisations provide valuable evidence of the
irresistible nature of the forces operating towards a
joint Anglo-American international currency on a
commodity standard.

According to the Ottawa Monetary Report and the
British Empire Currency Declaration, the world is
passing through a severe stage of currency deflation.
Reflation, that is the raising of the world wholesale
price level, is necessary until a position of equilibrium
is reached. The reflative progress actually achieved by
the Ottawa currency system was greatly hampered by
the operation of the gold standard. As stated:

For some months indeed it the [Ottawa Policy] had to
encounter obstacles arising from the continuance of a
downward trend in gold prices, and during that period the
results achieved were, in the main, limited to raising prices
in Empire currencies relative to gold prices.

However, thanks partly to the adoption of a currency
policy by the United States, based on principles
similar to those which formed the basis of the Ottawa
currency policy, more progress was achieved:

In the last few months the persistent adherence of the
United Kingdom to the policy of cheap and plentiful money
has been increasingly effective under the more favourable
conditions that have been created for the time being by the
change of policy of the United States and by the lull in
the fall of gold prices.

The actual result of the working of the Ottawa policy for a period of about twelve months is thus reported:

Taking the whole period, from June 29, 1932, just before the assembly of the Ottawa Conference, a rise in sterling wholesale prices has taken place of 12 per cent according to the *Economist* Index. The rise in the sterling prices of primary products during the same period has been much more substantial, being in the neighbourhood of 20 per cent.

Thus, whereas gold prices were falling, the Ottawa policy produced a substantial rise in sterling prices. This rise of prices was produced by "the persistent adherence of the United Kingdom to the policy of cheap and plentiful money." With the continued hoarding policy of the French Government, and the intensified hoarding by the peoples on the continent of Europe, Britain could not possibly have adhered to a policy of cheap and plentiful money if she had remained on a gold standard. A high bank rate would have been necessary to have prevented another drain of gold from the Bank of England. The Ottawa currency policy, on the contrary, made Britain independent of continental hoarding. The hoarders on the Continent could get as much gold as they wanted on paying the market price. The Bank of England could get as much gold as it wanted on paying the market price. But there was now no power to compel the Bank of England to sell gold to continental hoarders below market price, as in September 1931. The Ottawa currency policy had cured that form of monetary insanity. Britain was free to provide the internal industry of the country with all the currency and credit needed at cheap rates, because she was no longer compelled to protect her under-priced gold by a punitive bank rate.

Lord Bradbury's outburst against a Price Index as a standard of currency had made the delegates at the Ottawa Conference cautious about revealing the revolutionary nature of the currency system they were introducing. They knew, of course, that the rise in prices they repeatedly stressed could only be measured on a Price Index, but they were careful not to allow this knowledge to appear in their Report. But it was impossible for the British Empire Currency Declaration to report progress without doing so by means of a Price Index. The last passage quoted shows that the *Economist* Index of Wholesale Prices was chosen for this purpose. An attempt was made to use gold as the standard for measuring the rise in prices. But gold was ministering to the needs of hoarders rather than to the needs of commerce and industry. It showed a downward fall of prices rather than a rise. Gold had again failed. Just when the most urgent and insistent need for the return of the world to prosperity was a rise in the world wholesale price level, gold was pulling it down instead of assisting to raise it up.

The world has not yet arrived at the stage when prices can be stabilised. To apply the threefold tests which will in future be the criteria by which all policies of currency will be judged, industry and activity have not returned to normal; the producers of primary commodities are not yet ensured an economic return; and the burden of debts and fixed charges have not yet been harmonised with economic capacity. Progress is being made towards that stage, but progress must necessarily be slow in a world not yet unanimous as to the way to prosperity.

When that stage is attained, stability of prices will be effected by the same five methods of currency management as were used in managing the gold standard. Those methods were specified in Chapter IV. Instead of the movement of the bank rate being the first and the principal method, it will be used sparingly and only as a last resource when other methods have failed in securing the desired objective. Its effects on industry are too drastic for it to be used in the irresponsible manner associated with gold standard management. The Exchange Equalisation Fund has very greatly strengthened the Bank of England in its power to use the alternative methods of management, that is, open market operations and gold exchange methods. With its gold reserves supplemented by a Currency Management Fund of £350 millions, and with no obligation to sell gold below the market rate, the necessity for using the bank rate will arise only in most exceptional circumstances, if at all.

The stability of the international exchanges is recognised by the British Empire Currency Declaration as a problem still to be solved, as seen from the following passage:

The problem with which the world is faced is to reconcile the stability of exchange rates with a reasonable measure of stability not merely in the price level of a particular country, but in world prices.

The problem is, in fact, one of harmonising three stabilities, stability of the internal price level of each country; stability of the world wholesale price level; and stability of international exchange rates. The Declaration considers that the establishment of these three stabilities may need further sessions of the World Economic Conference, but affirms that substantial progress may in the meantime be effected by "the pursuit of a common policy of raising price levels" and "the adherence of other countries to a policy on similar lines." It is practically certain that no fresh sessions of the World Economic Conference will ever be called. Nor are they necessary. If only the British Empire Delegates had had more faith in their own currency system, as initiated at Ottawa, they would have seen that it leads inevitably to the harmony of the three stabilities. A further consideration on this issue is deferred to the next chapter.

In one respect the British Empire Currency Declaration makes a distinct advance on the Ottawa Currency System. The delegates at Ottawa, despite the strong lead given by the Macmillan Report, avoided any pronouncement on the vexed question of currency management. But twelve months' experience of the operation of the Exchange Equalisation Fund had removed all doubts about the necessity and the wisdom of currency management. At a time when a special fund of £350 millions was being devoted to currency management with complete success by the Bank of England, it was not necessary to be diffident about explaining its functions in the new currency system. The Declaration accordingly stated:

The Ottawa Conference declared that the ultimate aim of monetary policy must be the restoration of a satisfactory international monetary standard, having in mind not merely stable exchange rates between all countries, *but the deliberate management of the international standard*, in such a manner as to ensure the smooth and efficient working of international trade and finance.

A reference to Appendix I will demonstrate that the Ottawa Conference made no such declaration. The Ottawa Report did not contain the phrase:

but the deliberate management of the international standard.

As previously indicated, there was no time for careful revision of the Declaration before it was issued, and the phrase slipped out of its proper place in the hurry of the final compilation. It is unfortunate that this important phrase should have been misplaced. It indicates that the Ottawa currency system was intended to work as an international paper currency, independent of gold, but regulated and controlled by deliberate management. All the pretence of an automatic gold standard was brushed aside. The currency system initiated at Ottawa was actively functioning as an international paper currency. It was being deliberately managed by means of a Special Fund of £350 millions, with the objective of securing "the smooth and efficient working of international trade and finance."

One of the concluding paragraphs of the Declaration emphasises one of the results of the departure from the gold standard—the decline of the rate of interest on long-term loans. The delegates:

note with satisfaction the progress which has been made in that direction as well as in the resumption of oversea lending by the London Market. They agree that further advances on these lines will be beneficial as and when they can be made.

That suggestion has now be accepted. Further advances on these lines have actually been made. The resumption of oversea lending by the London Market has recently been extended not only to the nations of the British Commonwealth, but to those countries regulating their currencies in association with sterling. The common price policy of these countries is being recognised not only by stable exchange rates, but also by the extention of the privilege of participation in British loan facilities.

It is typical of the widespread ignorance of the currency policy of the British Government that, in the important Parliamentary Currency Debate on December 21, 1934, it was possible for Mr. Amery, a former Secretary of State for the Dominions, to make the following lamentable confession of being completely out of touch with the monetary situation:

What they were still asking for, and what they had not yet received, was a clear statement of the economic policy of the Government, and particularly their policy with regard to the monetary situation.

Mr. Neville Chamberlain, Chancellor of the Exchequer, was able to make the following telling reply:

We did declare our policy; indeed, the financial policy of the Empire, in terms at the conclusion of the London Conference. It has not materially changed in any respect since that declaration was made. I do not desire to alter what I have said about the desirability of raising wholesale prices. We have not been unsuccessful on the whole in our attempts to raise prices.

But not only was he able to state that the Ottawa currency policy, which had been reaffirmed at the conclusion of the World Economic Conference, had not been materially changed, and was operating with success; he went much further and announced the intention of the Government to continue this policy. Still more, he expressed the hope that this policy would do much to overcome the inharmonious elements of the currency systems of the world. The following quotation is of remarkable significance:

The prices of primary commodities have risen something like 30 per cent, and at the same time the cost of living has not gone up in this country. If we continue to pursue the policy, as laid down at the conclusion of the London Conference, and continue to produce the same results, I see no reason why we should not anticipate a further rise in the wholesale prices of primary commodities, which I think would do more to overcome the inharmonious elements which are to be found in the currency systems of the world to-day, than anything else.

Most significant of all, in his peroration, Mr. Neville Chamberlain carefully refrained from paying the customary tribute to the memory of the gold standard, and from expressing the hope for its resurrection, contenting himself with the following expression which would secure universal approval:

I look forward with confidence to the day when we shall be able once again to embark on an international currency standard.

The system inaugurated at Ottawa has now been in operation for over two years, and has coincided with a remarkable emergence of Britain from a long period of industrial stagnation and depression. No contrast can be more remarkable than that between the Britain of the gold standard period 1925 to 1931 and the Britain of the past two years. It is not mere coincidence. The Britain of 1932–34 has striking points of similarity with the Britain of a decade earlier, 1922–24. In both of these biennial periods Britain progressed from a period of depression towards an increasing prosperity. In both, the progress was due to the operation of a currency adapted to the prevailing conditions, an elastic currency free from the strangling and cramping bonds of the gold standard.

The prosperity of the earlier period was wilfully destroyed by a blind and doctrinaire recession to an obsolete and outworn system of currency. There is fortunately no reason to fear that the present return to prosperity will be jeopardised by a disastrous repetition of the great blunder of 1925.

During the printing of this volume, the Right Hon. Reginald McKenna has made his Annual Statement to the Shareholders of the Midland Bank. The following passages from his address, though too late to be incorporated into their appropriate positions in the text, harmonise so completely with the interpretation of British currency policy herein presented that the opportunity of inserting them should not be neglected. In particular, they give an authoritative refutation of Sir Josiah Stamp's interpretation of British currency policy quoted in the Foreword.

The following passage from Mr. McKenna's address sums up, in one pregnant sentence, the twelve chapters of this book:

The quantity of our money is no longer governed by the fortuitous supply of gold and the degree to which hoarding is practised by central banks and others; the quantity of money is subject now to pure management, with first regard to the needs of commerce and industry.

The strength and prestige of the currency systems initiated at Ottawa, the success it has achieved, and the suggestion of its permanent continuance, as stressed in the following passage, follow closely the lines of Mr. Neville Chamberlain's statement made in Parliament a month previously:

Now that sterling is free to find its own level in relation to foreign currencies the old restrictions on our power of development are removed, and there is no need for deflationary pressure to be put upon us as on the countries in the gold bloc. This holds true for the whole sterling group, which transacts a very large share of the world's trade and in which monetary policy has already brought about a substantial measure of recovery. It is difficult to find any reason why continuance of the monetary policy of the past three years should not yield equally favourable results.

That the gradual return of Britain and the nations of the Sterling Group to prosperity is directly attributable to the adoption of an alternative standard to gold, is implied in the following:

These facts illustrate very forcibly a striking benefit resulting from our departure from gold.

The revolutionary departure from the method of managing the gold standard, as described in the Cunliffe Report of 1918, is announced in the words:

Now, however, deflation, except as a corrective of internal inflation, has been banished as an unnecessary and discredited instrument of a freely operative monetary policy.

Finally, the improbability of Britain departing from the commodity standard which has restored her prosperity, since she adopted it at Ottawa, can be gathered from the following:

Accordingly, no reason can be found, either in the internal situation or in the position of our balance of payments, for reversing the monetary policy which has proved so successful in the past three years.

CHAPTER XII

THE CURRENCY REVOLUTION—
AND AFTER

"Mr. KEYNES: It would be a great advantage to any country to be able to work upon an international currency system, with local independence, would it not—That is what we would like for ourselves?

"Sir HENRY STRAKOSCH : Yes, but I do not see that that is feasible under the gold standard."—Extract from Evidence to the Macmillan Commission.

THE adoption of a gold standard by Britain in 1816 was not the result of a hastily considered decision. It was the result of a series of currency experiments which had extended over more than a century. The Newtonian experiments from 1700 to 1717; the stabilisation of the guinea at 21s.; the substitution of a virtual gold standard as the silver coinage drained away; the suspension of cash payments in 1797; all these were leading inevitably to the currency revolution of 1816, which established the gold standard till the outbreak of war in 1914.

The currency revolution of 1922–32 did not have the same degree of preparation. In the hurried days of reconstruction after the war it was necessary to improvise a new international currency, without an elaborate preparation. One flagrant defect of the gold standard was too obvious to be passed over. The gold standard had stabilised the monetary price of gold, but it had not stabilised its purchasing power. Its value in terms of money was fixed; its value in terms of goods and services fluctuated widely. The Genoa Conference of 1922, held at the instance of the League of Nations, assumed the general desirability of a return to a gold standard, but emphasised three principal objectives:

  i. each country to ensure the stability of its own currency.
 ii. the regulation of credit to keep national currencies at par with each other, that is, to keep the international exchanges stable.
iii. the regulation of credit to prevent undue fluctuations in the purchasing power of gold.

The second and third of these objectives had hitherto been considered as being incompatible with each other by orthodox economists and by bankers. The banking world repudiated the responsibility of regulating the purchasing power of gold, though the Cunliffe Report had demonstrated that the maintenance of stable exchanges involved violent interference with the purchasing power of currency. Stability of purchasing power had hitherto been generally regarded as being of far less importance than stability of the international exchanges.

The third objective, though adopted unanimously by thirty-three nations at Genoa, was never accepted by the Central Banks of the world. It was, however, adopted in the same year, 1922, on a national scale, by the Federal Reserve Board of the United States, under the leadership of Governor Strong. This was the first stage of the Currency Revolution, which took ten years to reach its final stage at Ottawa. At Genoa, it had been assumed that this objective could be attained without any departure from the traditional gold standard. But the moment it was attempted in practice, it was found that it involved a fundamental departure from the gold standard as previously operated. The change effected transformed the gold standard to such a degree that when Britain returned to the traditional gold standard in 1925, the currency policies of the two countries were involved in a conflict disastrous to both. The policy of Governor Strong having as its objective the stabilisation of the dollar, was, however, successful for six years, and was then abandoned, not because of any defects in its operation, but owing to a series of untoward circumstances.

The success it achieved during the six years of its operation had attracted much attention. It demonstrated that the policy of the Genoa Conference was practicable, and was far more suited to the industrial and commercial requirements of the post-war period than the gold standard. It proved that the elusive equilibrium-point between the evils of inflation and deflation was real and not imaginary. It added the term Reflation to the currency vocabulary. It proclaimed that Reflation was both the method and the objective of all sound currency management.

Meantime, the defects of the gold standard, and its unsuitability as an international currency in post-war conditions, were daily becoming more and more apparent. The Macmillan Commission in 1931 presented a Report recommending the complete transformation of the gold standard very much on the lines of the proposals of the Genoa Conference; or, in other words, the adoption of Governor Strong's dollar stabilisation policy on an international scale. The withdrawal of Britain from the gold standard in 1931 gave the British Empire Delegates at Ottawa a free hand in devising a new international currency system, an opportunity of which they availed themselves. They completed the Currency Revolution, initiated by Governor Strong, by adopting it for the nations of the British Commonwealth, by making it international instead of national, and by transforming it into a currency system that could be operated quite effectively on a paper basis, and that was quite independent of the return of the world to a gold standard.

Thus, the Ottawa currency system, initiated in 1932, expanded and completed the Currency Revolution, initiated by Governor Strong ten years previously. There was no organic connection between Governor Strong's dollar stabilisation system and the stabilisation of the world wholesale price level which is the main objective of the Ottawa currency system. But the two systems were two parts of one movement towards an international currency, adapted to post-war industrial and commercial conditions. They were both stimulated by the Genoa proposals to stabilise the purchasing power of gold. They were both practical efforts to correct one of the most glaring defects of the traditional gold standard, its neglect to stabilise purchasing power. The Ottawa system could never have been formulated with the precision and certainty that characterised the Ottawa Monetary Report, if it had not been for the knowledge and experience obtained from the practical working of the dollar stabilisation system for six years. They were not two separate revolutions, but two stages of the same revolution. The first stage was accomplished by the United States; the second stage was accomplished, and the revolution finished, by Britain. Without any conscious co-operation of the two countries, the currency revolution was, in effect, a co-operative achievement, each country making an essential contribution towards the end achieved.

The Ottawa Conference created an international currency system quite independent of gold, and then left the question of a return to gold open for discussion at the World Economic Conference. The partisans of a return to gold attempted to force the Conference back to a gold standard without any discussion of what had been achieved at Ottawa. They were repulsed, with the result that the revolution effected at Ottawa was confirmed by default. It continued as an international currency system on a paper basis, untroubled by a vague and un-meaning proviso for an ultimate return to gold, if certain impossible conditions should be fulfilled.

There is one point of resemblance between the present system of international currency established at Ottawa and the pre-war gold standard,—it is under

British control. The triple mismanagement of the international currency, by three countries operating three conflicting gold standards, has vanished. The remnant of the gold standard is gradually strangling the export trades of the countries of the gold bloc, and it is merely a question of time before they recognise their impossible situation and fall into line with the rest of the world. The United States is too much occupied with managing the purchasing power of the dollar to be able to devote much attention to the regulation and control of the international currency. As long as British currency policy is being conducted on the lines prescribed at Ottawa, it is in perfect harmony with President Roosevelt's dollar policy. The United States is not likely to question Britain's control of the international currency, so long as it is in harmony with the internal currency policy of the United States.

British control of the international currency is being effected by means of the Exchange Equalisation Fund. The United States has an Exchange Equalisation Fund of greater dimensions than the British Fund, but, as will be seen from Appendix IV, it is not being actively used; and Dr. Sprague is not at all certain that it will be used in the foreign exchange market; whereas the British Fund is actively used up to the last pound for the purpose of keeping the international exchanges as stable as conditions will permit.[1]

The United States can intervene in international

[1] But see Supplementary Note on p. 242.

currency by changing the gold content of the dollar. But such interventions are spasmodic. Their primary intention is to influence the internal price level. Not being continuous they do not partake of the nature of the management or control of the international currency. The difference between British control and the occasional intervention of the United States is well illustrated by the following quotation from Mr. Rand:

> Through the period of gold hoarding and panic, British confidence has been rebuilt and sustained, although it has been necessary to change the price of gold in London almost every day. Instead of frightening British investors and British industry, this policy has increased bank prices, intensified business velocity, stabilised values generally, and brought the most active house-building development England has ever experienced.

The true relationship between a national currency and the international standard is expressed by the query of Mr. Keynes at the heading of this chapter, national independence, but a workable association with the international currency. The reply of Sir Henry Strakosch is equally significant. That relationship is impossible on a gold standard.

Mr. Keynes elaborates his conception of that relationship between a national currency with the international standard in his *Treatise on Money* in the following passages:

> The dilemma of an international system (is) to preserve the advantages of the stability of the local currencies in terms of the international standard, and to preserve at the same time an adequate local autonomy for each member.

and:

The solution is to be sought by arranging some compromise in virtue of which adherence to an international standard is combined in a regular and legitimate way with a reasonable measure of local autonomy.

He discusses this solution at length, on a gold standard basis, but also states that, apart from a gold standard, progress towards his conception of an international currency associated with independent national currencies could be effected in three stages:

   i. The release of national currencies from the inconvenient and sometimes dangerous obligation of being tied to an unmanaged international system.
   ii. The evolution of independent national currencies with fluctuating exchange rates.
  iii. The linking of these national currencies into a managed international system.

These three stages bear some resemblance to the Ottawa system of currency. The first stage has already been completed for all countries which have withdrawn from the mismanaged gold standard. The second and third stages are proceeding simultaneously, independent national currencies linking themselves to the managed international currency—Sterling, which is being deliberately managed, in the words of the British Empire Currency Declaration, "in such a manner as to ensure the smooth and efficient working of international trade and finance." The fluctuating exchange rates of the second stage are being evened down by the common price policies of the participating countries.

The working of the Ottawa currency system is proceeding somewhat on the following lines. Each participating country is regulating its internal currency according to purely national requirements. It is attempting to stabilise its internal price level, as measured by its own National Consumption Standard, or Cost of Living Index; and, at the same time, doing its utmost to raise the world wholesale price level. The wide discrepancy between wholesale and retail prices renders this quite a feasible policy. Britain is co-operating by using its outstanding international position, backed by the Exchange Equalisation Fund, to cause a steady rise in the world wholesale price level. The common price policies, though not as yet producing absolute stability of exchange rates between the participating countries, reduces the fluctuations to small dimensions.

The best practical illustration of this system is the relation between the Krona, the national currency of Sweden, and Sterling, the international currency. Sweden has adopted a krona stabilisation policy, almost exactly similar to Governor Strong's dollar stabilisation policy in operation in the United States from 1922–28. The results have been, on the whole, satisfactory, even though the Swedish financial system was shaken to its foundations by the Kreuger crisis. But the internal stabilisation of the krona did not prevent a comparative stabilisation of the krona with sterling. There have been fluctuations between the two currencies, especially during the confusion after they had both withdrawn from the gold standard. But these discrepancies gradually evened down, and, though the return to a protection policy on the part of Britain has been a great blow to the Swedish export trade, it has not caused undue fluctuations in the exchange rate between the two countries.

That is the Ottawa currency system in actual operation. It is as yet in its initial stages, and represents only the first crude efforts of both countries to pull themselves out of the slough of depression into which they were dragged by the gold standard. Experience will suggest many methods by which any want of harmony between national and international interests which may manifest itself may be minimised. It demonstrates that Mr. Keynes' ideal, an independent local currency, with a workable association with an international currency, is not a dream but an actually realised fact. There is no suggestion of dependence or of subordinating Swedish national interests to external forces. The Swedish krona is perfectly independent, and is managed entirely by the Swedish Riksbank to serve Swedish interests. It is associated with sterling only so far as it serves the interest of Swedish international commerce to be closely associated with an international currency.

One of the most interesting currency problems of the day is the question whether the Ottawa system provides the possibility of harmonising the currency interests of Britain and the United States. President Roosevelt's aims and objectives are identical with those of the Ottawa system; but his methods, in particular the modification of the gold content of the dollar, differ from those adopted by Britain. But the modification of the gold content of the dollar is not a method that is likely to be repeated frequently or indefinitely. There may be one, possibly two, conceivably three, changes in the gold content of the dollar before it is regarded as having found its natural level. To the American mind the gold content of the pound is changed with every change in the sterling price of gold. But there is a difference between the change in the price of a paper unit, which has no gold content, and is merely following the normal movements of the gold market, and an intended change in the gold content of the dollar, a unit which has always been regarded as an actual coin.

Although Britain and the United States are pursuing identical policies, active co-operation will not be necessary until the gold content of the dollar has attained some degree of fixity. Co-operation will then be facilitated by the fact that while the United States is primarily interested in the internal purchasing power of the dollar, the international currency policies of both countries are the same.

As soon as the period of crisis has passed, the United States will probably return to Governor Strong's policy and methods of dollar stabilisation. The Federal Reserve Board will, in all probability, be reformed and strengthened in order to give it much greater unity and promptitude in action, and a much stricter control over the banking system and the creation of bank money.

But, though the stabilisation of the dollar is purely a national question, the interest of the United States in the external purchasing power of the dollar will suggest some degree of co-operation with Britain. The prices of agricultural products exported, and of the raw materials imported, are governed by the world price level, and not by the internal purchasing power of the dollar. If the stable purchasing power of the dollar is to have a uniform effect over the whole country, it is essential that the prices of agricultural products shall remain at a level commensurate with that of industrial products, and this objective can be achieved only by exercising some control over the world price level.

The problem of harmonising complete independence of the internal purchasing power of the dollar with a certain degree of co-operation with Britain in managing its external purchasing power can be achieved by the use of two Price Indexes. For internal purposes the United States will naturally continue to use its internal Wholesale Price Index giving the weighted average of over seven hundred commodities and services in general demand. The dollar will eventually be stabilised internally on that Price Index.

For International purposes a different price index, probably the Production Index of the League of Nations, would be used. It would have to be decided by the international co-operation of the United States, the nations of the British Commonwealth, and the nations regulating their currency in association with sterling. Each nation will utilise its own national Consumption Index for regulating its national currency, but the international currency would have to be regulated on some mutually agreed Price Index of an international character.

The time for such a Conference will not arise until the rise in world wholesale prices will have reached such a level that stabilisation is considered possible. The British Empire Currency Declaration has stated the three fundamental conditions that must be satisfied before stabilisation should be attempted. Provided that these conditions have been satisfied, the Conference would have very definite issues to settle, the actual Price Index to be used for the standard of International Currency, the equilibrium point on that Index to be selected as the actual standard, the amount of divergence from the standard to be permitted before corrective action is considered necessary, and the uniform action to be taken should the world wholesale price level tend to escape from the prescribed limits. This method would entail the minimum of interference with the independence of each nation in regulating its internal price level, and secure co-operative action in regulating the world wholesale price level.

It is possible that such a Conference might leave the day-to-day management of the International currency to Britain, having determined the general principles by which such management should be conducted. Britain will probably be the only country regulating its internal currency on the same Price Level as that on which the international currency is regulated. Other countries will have their own Consumer's Index as their currency standards. Britain will have one Index, probably the Production Index of the League of Nations, for the currency standard on which the value of the pound sterling, both internal and external, will be regulated. Moreover, Britain is the only country willing to allow its Central Bank reserves, the gold reserve at the Bank of England, and the Exchange Equalisation Fund, to be used solely and entirely for international currency management. Other countries require their Central Bank reserves to be utilised as a backing for their internal currency in order to secure a high degree of convertibility. Britain has no such use for its reserves.

Other countries, finding Britain with an international currency, sterling, already in active working order, and finding Britain willing to undertake the heavy responsibilities of managing this international currency, and to provide the enormous fund necessary for its management, may leave Britain, at any rate for the time being, to manage sterling as an international currency on generally agreed principles. To what extent this arrangement will be permanent will depend on the success with which it works, and the degree to which the internal currencies of the various countries are able, without any undue stress or loss of independence, to maintain an equilibrium with sterling so managed.

It has been contended, in opposition to this currency system, that there is no guarantee, or even any likelihood, of the nationally controlled currencies, each operated on a Consumers' Price Index, keeping in equilibrium with an international currency, operated on a Production Price Index. It is pointed out that the standard of living of no two countries is alike. Consequently their consumption price levels will not necessarily keep step with each other on their respective Price Indexes. Still less will they keep in step with the movements of the world wholesale price level measured on a wholesale production price index.

After considering this point in his *Treatise on Money*, Mr. Keynes comes to the following conclusion:

> The long-period variability of local Consumption Standards or Earning Standards, in terms of a stable International Standard, is not likely to be so large as to matter much to economic well-being.

This conclusion is supported by actual experience of the working of the Ottawa system of currency. Local currencies based on local standards, as in Sweden, are keeping in general equilibrium with the international currency, sterling. There are greater discrepancies between sterling and the local currencies of Australia and New Zealand, but these date from a period prior to the Ottawa Conference. The discrepancies are not the result of the operation of the Ottawa system. They are due to prior causes. The Ottawa system has prevented these discrepancies from widening to still more divergent limits.

The Ottawa currency system propounds a solution to the problem of harmonising the three stabilities:

 i. the stability of the internal price level,
 ii. the stability of the world wholesale price level,
 iii. the stability of the international exchanges.

They are stabilities to be produced naturally by the common interests and the common price policies of the participating nations; not artificial stabilities based on the selection of a single commodity, gold, as a fulcrum for working the levers of currency management. The system is as yet in its initial stages. It is doubtful whether, even in the City of London, there is more than a small percentage of bankers and financiers who are aware that it is operating. It is supported only by a proportion of the nations of the world. It is regarded with intense hostility by the nations of the gold bloc. Naturally, in such circumstances, its achievements so far are not equal to its possibilities.

Moreover, discrepancies and fluctuations are more likely to creep in during the initial stage of raising world wholesale prices than in the subsequent stages when world wholesale prices will have attained an equilibrium and have been stabilised. The task of raising world prices, after a prolonged downward monetary movement for several years, and in the teeth of the opposition of the countries of the gold bloc, is so colossal that in itself it tends to produce fluctuations and movements in other directions. It will not be till this task is accomplished that the efficiency of the Ottawa system in smoothing out fluctuations and disturbances of the three stabilities essential to world prosperity can be judged. It is facing its most difficult task, that of raising world price levels, while it is still in its infancy. If it succeeds in this initial task, its subsequent problems should not be beyond its mature strength to solve.

There is a fourth stability, the stability of the purchasing power of gold, with which the new currency system is only indirectly concerned. The purchasing power of gold is now not strictly a currency problem. It is determined much more by hoarding, and by the desire for the convertibility of the currency into gold, than by the currency usage of gold. Until the Ottawa system has passed through its experimental stage, and established itself as a universally acknowledged currency system, the price and the purchasing power of gold will be indeterminate. As seen in Chapter X, gold will still perform many essential currency functions, even though it may never again be the international currency standard. The greater its stability in price and in purchasing power, the more valuable will be its currency services.

The craze for hoarding is associated with a misconception concerning the possibility of converting paper money into gold. Modern industry and commerce require a volume of currency that cannot possibly be provided by the amount of gold and silver available for currency purposes. Except in primitive communities, paper money must supplement gold and silver to such an extent that complete convertibility is impossible. Complete convertibility would reduce commerce and industry to the limited range that could be financed by a purely metallic currency. Convertibility is an ever threatening deflative force, latent in normal times, but which comes into action in times of crisis, and is then capable of bringing the strongest currency system down to the ground. The price and the purchasing power of gold can never be stable, as long as there exists a belief in the unlimited convertibility of paper money.

The world is gradually getting used to an inconvertible international currency,—sterling. But most nations will not be satisfied with an inconvertible national currency. They will attempt to create a belief in the convertibility of their national currencies by keeping as large reserves of gold as they can afford. The purchasing power of gold is not, therefore, susceptible to currency management. It is dominated by two purely psychological forces, the demand for hoarding and the demand for convertibility. These forces can neither be measured nor estimated, and it is very doubtful how far they can be controlled.

The principal cause of the failure of the Genoa Conference was that it under-rated the psychological forces regulating the price and purchasing power of gold. It imagined that the astonishing success of the Bank of England in regulating the price of gold for ninety-two years could be repeated in a post-war world which had already shown signs of a reversion to hoarding. It imagined that one exceptionally difficult feat, possible only to a country with the peculiar freedom of the British mentality from the metallic complex, would be performed, as a matter of course, by nations possessed by a passionate desire for hoarding gold. The Central Banks who were exhorted by the Genoa Conference to take measures to avoid undue fluctuations in the purchasing power of gold were themselves seized with the hoarding complex which defeated the aims of the Conference.

The Ottawa currency system wisely avoided that inscrutable problem—the stabilisation of the purchasing power of gold. The Ottawa delegates were concerned primarily with currency, not with hoarding, not with convertibility. They were aware that the purchasing power of gold was determined by these two factors which were outside the range of their deliberations. They therefore devised a currency system free from that incalculable factor, the purchasing power of gold. The purchasing power of paper is a calculable factor. It follows definite laws. It is free from the superstition and variable psychology attaching to gold. As such it is an ideal medium for an international currency.

Gold has its currency uses. In particular it can settle international balances, in so far as they are not settled by the mutual exchanges of goods and services. These can be settled by gold as a commodity with a variable market price, as easily as if it were a currency at a fixed price. Other uses of gold may be monetary uses, but they are not currency uses. Currency implies circulation. Hoarding is not a currency use. It is the devotion of currency to an alien use. Convertibility is only a currency factor in so far as it inspires confidence. The moment convertibility is actually exercised, it means an addition to hoarding and a loss to currency.

The fourth form of stability—the stability of the purchasing power of gold—is the fifth wheel of the currency coach. Only three forms of currency stability are essential to commerce and industry:

The stability of the internal currency,
The stability of the world wholesale price level,
The stability of the international exchanges.

The Ottawa currency system is a system by means of which these three stabilities can be secured independently of gold. Should any nation, in addition to these three stabilities, desire the luxury of convertibility, it can create the illusion of convertibility by the size of its gold reserves. It can never attain complete convertibility. But it is one of the characteristices of the gold complex that it is normally satisfied with the illusion of convertibility, and only seeks the reality of the possession of gold in times of crisis.

The most serious criticism of the Ottawa currency system and of President Roosevelt's policy of the stable dollar was expressed in advance in the Macmillan Report in the following passage:

We have said that the ultimate aim should be the stability of the international price level, meaning by this the composite price at wholesale of the principal foodstuffs and raw materials entering into international trade as measured by the best-known wholesale index numbers. Difficult problems will no doubt arise as to whether any particular fall in prices is due to a greater ease or efficiency of production, and different views may be taken as to whether such changes should be counteracted by monetary influences. The general price level, for instance, might fall because of a heavy fall in the price of one commodity; e.g. wheat or cotton. Are Central Banks to attempt to counteract this influence by a general rise in other prices?

That query expresses the criticism of the policy of the absolute stabilisation of prices at a fixed level, advanced by many modern economists, among whom may be mentioned Robertson, Hawtrey and the Coles. They suggest that the correct currency standard should be an "Earnings" or "Cost of Production" standard, rather than a fixed Price Index standard. This standard was strongly presented to the United States House of Representatives Sub-Committee on Banking and Currency by Mr. Rufus S. Tucker of the Brookings Institution of Washington. The following is a selection from his evidence:

The index of wholesale prices is not, in my opinion, the proper thing to stabilise, because, if wholesale prices were stabilised, that would require that all other kinds of prices would rise very rapidly.

If you will analyse these prices you will find the agricultural prices had gone down, while some others had gone up.

Dennis Robertson, of England, has come out emphatically in that direction, and has pointed out a very important theoretical consideration, to the effect that for the last century or so improvements have been going on in methods of production, and the reduction of costs has been estimated to average about 3 per cent a year. Consequently, he maintains that the wholesale price index ought to decline 3 per cent a year, the reason being that that is the only way in which benefits of improved technique can be divided among the people at large.

A superficial answer to such a criticism is that a decline of 3 per cent per annum in the wholesale price level would bring about a deflation more severe than was ever effected by any gold standard. Mr. Robertson would probably disclaim the drastic practical proposals of his American admirer.

The correct reply to this criticism is that the "Earnings" or "Cost of Production" standard is essentially a local or national standard, and not suitable for adoption as the basis of an international currency standard. Earnings and costs of production differ so widely in different countries that it would be impossible to work out a suitable Earnings or Cost of Production Index that would serve as the basis of an international currency and be fair to all countries. It is not till the varied earnings and the diverse costs of production of the various countries of the world have been evened out into the world wholesale prices of commodities, that they can form a basis for an international currency.

It is quite possible, and it may prove to be quite feasible, that certain countries may prefer to adopt an Earnings or a Cost of Production Standard as the basis of their respective national currencies. Experience can only decide whether such national currencies would be in harmony with an international standard based on the Production Index of the League of Nations.

Without in any way ruling out the future possibility of an international Earnings or Cost of Production Standard, the most probable course of currency development will be the general adoption of the Price Index Standard, inaugurated at Ottawa as the basis of an international currency, with experimental excursions into other standards by individual countries in accordance with their national interests.

An independent revolutionary effect of the Ottawa policy is at present only in its initial stages. Reference has already been made in previous chapters to the widespread criticism of the banking system, on the grounds that it has usurped the functions of the State in creating bank money, and that it has failed to administer such created bank money in the true interests of the community. The Ottawa currency system is an elementary assertion of the authority of the Government over the issue and operation of bank money. Never again will the Bank of England be able to disorganise the industry and commerce of the country by raising the bank rate unduly for the purposes of international finance. "Low rates of interest," "an abundance of short-term money" and the keeping of the rate of interest for all purposes "as low as financial conditions permit," have been prescribed, and will be enforced with the whole weight of the Governments of the nations of the British Commonwealth. The discretion of the Bank of England in the operation of the bank rate is severely limited by the Ottawa currency system. Whether the success which the Ottawa policy has already achieved will stimulate the Government to consider the remainder of the criticisms levied at the banking system, and establish a still stricter control over the issue of bank money, remains to be seen. In particular the maintenance of the minimum rate of 5 per cent for loans to internal industry and commerce, in contrast with a bank rate of 2 per cent, is a feature of the present banking system which inspires the strongest criticism.

It is not, however, in any particular direction, but in the general insistence that monetary policy must for the future be devoted primarily to the service of industry and commerce, that the freedom of the banks in the control of bank money will be curtailed. Remunerative prices, stable prices, the efficient working of the machinery of international trade and finance—these are to be the objectives of future currency policy. In so far as the banks further these objectives they may be permitted to escape further control. But the slightest attempt on the part of the banking system to depart from them will entail an almost irresistible call for greater control of their operations by Government.

It is manifestly impossible to give more than a tentative description of the operation of a currency system so shortly after it has been inaugurated. But of more importance than the description of the new currency system is the fact that a currency revolution has actually happened. It is but a few months since (April—May 1934) that a prolonged correspondence appeared in *The Times*, in which it was urged that the

Government should appoint a Commission to inquire into the currency system in operation, and to make recommendations for a new currency system adapted to modern requirements. The correspondents included personages eminent in the worlds of currency, finance and commerce. And yet they, one and all, appeared to be completely ignorant that the currency revolution most of them desired had actually been effected. Their currency knowledge appeared to end with the Macmillan Report, read in a slovenly and superficial manner. They dismissed it as being completely out-of-date, because it had recommended the retention of the gold standard. They had no conception of Lord Bradbury's description of its revolutionary nature. They were completely oblivious of the revolutionary currency system initiated at Ottawa. They appeared to be equally oblivious of the fact that there had been a British Empire Currency Declaration, after the breakdown of the World Economic Conference, describing a revolutionary system of currency, actually in being, as the official policy of the British Empire.

Yet a Currency Revolution, as thorough and as outstanding as the adoption of the gold standard in 1816, had taken place under their very noses. The Revolution was so stupendous that Lord Bradbury had stated that it would not even come within the range of practical international politics during the lifetime of the youngest of us. It had not only come within range, it had been transmuted into an actively working international currency system, barely twelve months after Lord Bradbury's prophecy. Shortly before the correspondence mentioned, *The Times* had scared its readers with details of some so-called revolutionary proposals made by President Roosevelt. Yet, when they came to be examined they were found to be a moderate variant of the official currency policy adopted by the British Empire. President Roosevelt's message to the World Economic Conference, July 3, 1933, was supposed to enunciate such advanced and revolutionary currency doctrines that it caused the Conference to break up in confusion. And yet he had merely re-stated the policy which had been adopted eleven months before at Ottawa as the official British currency system.

The final chapter of a previous volume published by the author[1] contained a brief description of the currency revolution recently effected at Ottawa, and confirmed by the British Empire Currency Declaration, issued after the breakdown of the World Economic Conference. No sooner had the nature of this revolution been brought to the notice of the "Committee for the Nation" in the United States than it proceeded to ask indignantly:

> Why did Mr. James P. Warburg, whom President Roosevelt sent to represent the United States at the London Economic Conference, not publish the story of what England was doing?

The Committee of the Nation immediately proceeded to publish the story of what England was doing with

[1] *The Rise and Fall of the Gold Standard.*

the whole power of its wonderful organisation. It is quite certain that the United States knows what England is doing, and what England has done, to bring the international currency system into harmony with modern requirements, far better than England herself knows it. It is with the hope that it may bring to the consciousness of the people of Britain some knowledge of the magnificent achievement of Britain in devising a system of currency that is actively operating to rescue the world from the despair and depression of the past decade that this volume has been written.

SUPPLEMENTARY NOTE.—It is necessary to revise the statement that there is doubt whether the United States Exchange Equalisation Fund will be used. On February 11, 1935, Mr. Morgenthau, Secretary to the Treasury, announced that the Fund had been used in foreign exchange markets to manage the value of the dollar since January 14, 1935. The occasion for its use was the instability due to the uncertainty as to the decision of the Supreme Court on the validity of the Gold Clause.

THE OTTAWA MONETARY REPORT

Report of the Committee on Monetary and Financial Questions of the Ottawa Conference, adopted by the Full Conference.

1. (*a*) A rise throughout the world in the general levels of wholesale prices is in the highest degree desirable. The evil of falling prices must be attacked by Government and individual action in all its causes, which are political, economic, financial, or monetary.

(*b*) For dealing with the problem in its widest aspect the Governments represented at this Conference record their conviction that international action is urgently necessary and announce their desire to co-operate with other nations in any practicable measures for raising wholesale prices.

(*c*) The Conference has considered what action can be taken by nations of the Commonwealth to help towards raising prices.

As regards monetary action, the Conference recognises that the central position of the United Kingdom, not only among countries of the Commonwealth but in world trade and finance, makes the United Kingdom a main factor in anything that can be done. The Conference therefore welcomes the following statement made on behalf of the United Kingdom by the Chancellor of the Exchequer:

His Majesty's Government desires to see wholesale sterling prices rise. The best condition for this would be a rise in gold prices, and the absence of a rise in gold prices inevitably imposes limitations on what can be done for sterling. A rise in prices cannot be effected by monetary action, since various other factors which have combined to bring about the present depression must also be modified or removed before a remedy is assured. His Majesty's Government nevertheless recognises that an ample supply of short-term money at low rates may have a valuable influence, and they are confident that the efforts which have successfully brought about the present favourable monetary conditions can and will, unless unforeseen difficulties arise, be continued.

(*d*) The Conference recommends the other countries of the Commonwealth represented here to act in conformity with the line of policy as set out in the statement of the Chancellor of the Exchequer so far as lies within their power.

In the monetary sphere the primary line of action towards a rise in prices should be the creation and maintenance, within the limits of sound finance, of such conditions as will assist the revival of enterprise and trade. Among these conditions are low rates of interest and an abundance of short-term money. While regard must be had to the different conditions applying to the various types of loans, the rate of interest for all purposes should be kept as low as financial conditions permit.

At the same time it is necessary that these favourable monetary conditions be achieved, not by the inflationary creation of additional means of payment to finance public expenditure, but by an orderly monetary policy, safeguarded, if necessity should arise, by such steps as will restrain and circumscribe the scope of violent speculative movements in commodities or securities.

It must be kept in mind, however, that the success of any such policy will be hampered, and might be nullified, by failure to modify or remove important non-monetary obstacles. Of non-monetary factors which are depressing the level of prices many are of international character and require an international remedy. The nations of the Commonwealth should nevertheless take all steps that lie in their power to increase public confidence, especially in the field of business enterprise, and to facilitate trade.

(*e*) The Conference recognises the great importance to traders of stability of exchange rates over as wide an area as possible. The complete solution òf this problem must await the restoration of conditions for the satisfactory working of an international standard, as referred to below. In the meanwhile, and pending such a solution, this Conference has considered the possibility of achieving valuable results in two directions—first, by creating an area of stability among countries regulating their currencies in relation to sterling; and, secondly, by avoiding wide day-to-day fluctuations between sterling and gold.

APPENDIX

As regards the latter, the Conference has noted with satisfaction that the United Kingdom has already established machinery aiming at preventing wide fluctuations in gold value of sterling caused by speculative movements. As to the former, the Conference recognises the value of countries within the Commonwealth whose currencies are linked to sterling maintaining stability between their exchange rates, and looks to a rise in the general level of wholesale prices as the most desirable means for facilitating this result.

2. The Conference recognises that the ultimate aim of monetary policy should be the restoration of a satisfactory international monetary standard. Such a standard should so function as not merely to maintain stable exchanges between all countries, but also to ensure the smooth and efficient working of the machinery of international trade and finance.

This postulates international agreement among the great trade nations of the world, and, while certain of the States here represented hold very definite views on the question of the most desirable standard, the Conference refrains from making any recommendation on the subject, in view of the fact that the question is shortly to be discussed at an international conference.

There are, however, several conditions precedent to the re-establishment of any international monetary standard. The most important among them are: A rise in the general level of commodity prices in various countries to a height more in keeping with the level of costs, including the burden of debts and other fixed and semi-fixed charges; and an adjustment of factors, political, economic, financial, and monetary, which have caused the breakdown of the gold standard in many countries, and which, if not adjusted, would inevitably lead to another breakdown of whatever international standard may be adopted.

It is also, in the view of the Conference, of the utmost importance to the future working of any international standard that international co-operation should be secured and maintained, with a view to avoiding, so far as may be found practicable, wide fluctuations in the purchasing power of standards of value.

THE BRITISH EMPIRE CURRENCY
DECLARATION

*Declaration of the Delegates of the United Kingdom and
the Nations of the British Commonwealth, issued on
July 27, 1933, at the close of the World Economic
Conference.*

1. Now that the World Economic and Monetary Conference has adjourned, the undersigned delegations of the
British Commonwealth consider it appropriate to put on
record their views on some of the more important matters
of financial and monetary policy which were raised but not
decided at the Conference. During the course of the Conference they have had the opportunity of consulting together
and reviewing, in the light of present-day conditions, the
conclusions arrived at at their meeting at Ottawa a year ago,
in so far as they had reference to the issues before the
Conference.

2. The undersigned delegations are satisfied that the
Ottawa Agreements have already had beneficial effects on
many branches of inter-Imperial trade and that this process
is likely to continue as the purchasing power of the various
countries concerned increases. While there has not yet been
sufficient time to give full effect to the various agreements
made, they are convinced that the general principles agreed
upon are sound. The undersigned delegations reaffirm their
conviction that the lowering or removal of barriers between
the countries of the Empire provided for in the Ottawa
Agreements will not only facilitate the flow of goods between
them, but will stimulate and increase the trade of the world.

3. The delegations now desire to draw attention to the
principles of monetary and financial policy which have
emerged from the work of both the Ottawa and World
Conferences, and which are of the utmost importance for
the countries within the British Commonwealth. The

following paragraphs embody their views as to the principles
of policy which they consider desirable for their countries.

4. At the Ottawa Conference the Governments represented declared their view that a rise throughout the world
in the general level of wholesale prices was in the highest
degree desirable, and stated that they were anxious to
co-operate with other nations in any practicable measures
for raising wholesale prices. They agreed that a rise in prices
could not be effected by monetary action alone, since various
other factors which combined to bring about the present
depression must also be modified or removed before a
remedy is assured.

It was indicated that international action would be needed
to remove the various non-monetary factors which were
depressing the level of prices.

In the monetary sphere the primary line of action towards
a rise in prices was stated to be the creation and maintenance within the limits of sound finance of such conditions
as would assist in the revival of enterprise and trade, including
low rates of interest and an abundance of short-term money.
The inflationary creation of additional means of payment
to finance public expenditure was deprecated, and an orderly
monetary policy was demanded with safeguards to limit the
scope of violent speculative movements of commodities and
securities.

5. Since then the policy of the British Commonwealth
has been directed to raising prices. The undersigned
delegations note with satisfaction that this policy has been
attended with an encouraging measure of success. For some
months indeed it had to encounter obstacles arising from
the continuance of a downward trend of gold prices, and
during that period the results achieved were in the main
limited to raising prices in Empire currencies relatively to
gold prices. In the last few months the persistent adherence
of the United Kingdom to the policy of cheap and plentiful
money has been increasingly effective under the more
favourable conditions that have been created for the time
being by the change of policy of the United States, and by
the halt in the fall of gold prices.

Taking the whole period from June 29, 1932, just before the assembly of the Ottawa Conference, a rise in sterling wholesale prices has taken place of 12 per cent according to the *Economist* index. The rise in the sterling prices of primary products during the same period has been much more substantial, being in the neighbourhood of 20 per cent.

6. The undersigned delegations are of opinion that the views they expressed at Ottawa as to the necessity of a rise in the price level still hold good, and that it is of the greatest importance that this rise which has begun should continue. As to the ultimate level to be aimed at they do not consider it practicable to state this in precise terms. Any price level would be satisfactory which restores the normal activity of industry and employment, which ensures an economic return to the producer of primary commodities, and which harmonises the burden of debts and fixed charges with economic capacity. It is important that the rise in prices should not be carried to such a pitch as to produce an inflated scale of profits, and threaten a disturbance of equilibrium in the opposite direction. They therefore consider that the Governments of the British Commonwealth should persist by all means in their power, whether monetary or economic, within the limits of sound finance in the policy of furthering the rise in wholesale prices until there is evidence that equilibrium has been re-established, and that thereupon they should take whatever measures are possible to stabilise the position thus attained.

7. With reference to the proposal which has been made from time to time for the expansion of Government programmes of capital outlay, the British Commonwealth delegations consider that this is a matter which must be dealt with by each Government in the light of its own experience, and of its own conditions.

8. The Ottawa Conference declared that the ultimate aim of monetary policy must be the restoration of a satisfactory international monetary standard, having in mind, not merely stable exchange rates between all countries, but the deliberate management of the international standard in such a manner as to ensure the smooth and efficient

working of international trade and finance. The principal conditions precedent to the re-establishment of any international monetary standard were stated, particularly a rise in the general level of commodity prices in the various countries, to a height more in keeping with the level of costs, including the burden of debt and other fixed and semi-fixed charges, and the Conference expressed its sense of the importance of securing and maintaining international co-operation with a view to avoiding, so far as may be found practicable, wide fluctuations in the purchasing power of the standard of value.

9. The undersigned delegations now reaffirm their view that the ultimate aim of monetary policy should be the restoration of a satisfactory international gold standard, under which international co-operation would be secured and maintained, with a view to avoiding, so far as may be found practicable, undue fluctuations in the purchasing power of gold. The problem with which the world is faced is to reconcile the stability of exchange rates with a reasonable measure of stability, not merely in the price level of a particular country, but in world prices. Effective action in this matter must largely depend on international co-operation, and in any further sessions of the World Economic and Monetary Conference this subject must have special prominence.

10. In the meantime the undersigned delegations recognise the importance of stability of exchange rates between the countries of the Empire in the interests of trade. This objective will be constantly kept in mind in determining their monetary policy, and its achievement will be aided by the pursuit of a common policy of raising price levels. Inter-Imperial stability of exchange rates is facilitated by the fact that the United Kingdom Government has no commitments to other countries as regards the future management of sterling and retains complete freedom of action in this respect. The adherence of other countries to a policy on similar lines would make possible the attainment and maintenance of exchange stability over a still wider area.

11. Among the factors working for the economic recovery

of the countries of the Commonwealth, special importance attaches to the decline in the rate of interest on long-term loans. The undersigned delegations note with satisfaction the progress which has been made in that direction as well as in the resumption of oversea lending by the London market. They agree that further advances on these lines will be beneficial as and when they can be made.

12. The undersigned delegations have agreed that they will recommend their Governments to consult with one another from time to time on monetary and economic policy with a view to establishing their common purpose and to the framing of such measures as may conduce towards its achievement.

The declaration has not been signed by the representative of the Irish Free State, who has referred the matter to his Government.

UNITED STATES CURRENCY POLICY

Message of President Roosevelt to the World Economic Conference sent on July 3, 1933.

I WOULD regard it as a catastrophe amounting to a world tragedy if the great Conference of nations, called to bring about a more real and permanent financial stability and a greater prosperity to the masses of all nations, should, in advance of any serious effort to consider these broader problems, allow itself to be diverted by the proposal of a purely artificial and temporary experiment affecting the monetary exchange of a few nations only. Such action, such diversion, shows a singular lack of proportion and a failure to remember the larger purposes for which the Economic Conference originally was called together.

I do not relish the thought that insistence on such action should be made an excuse for the continuance of the basic economic errors that underlie so much of the present world-wide depression.

The world will not long be lulled by the specious fallacy of achieving a temporary and probably an artificial stability in foreign exchange on the part of a few large countries only.

The sound internal economic system of a nation is a greater factor in its well-being than the price of its currency in changing terms of the currencies of other nations.

It is for this reason that reduced cost of Government, adequate Government income, and ability to service Government debts are all so important to ultimate stability. So, too, old fetishes of so-called international bankers are being replaced by efforts to plan national currencies with the objective of giving to those currencies a continuing purchasing power which does not greatly vary in terms of the commodities and need of modern civilisation. Let me be frank in saying that the United States seeks the kind of a dollar which a generation hence will have the same purchasing and debt-paying power as the dollar value we hope to attain in the near future. That objective means more to the good of other nations than a fixed ratio for a month or two in terms of the pound or franc.

Our broad purpose is the permanent stabilisation of every nation's currency. Gold or gold and silver can well continue to be a metallic reserve behind currencies, but this is not the time to dissipate gold reserves. When the world works out concerted policies in the majority of nations to produce balanced budgets, and living within their means, then we can properly discuss a better distribution of the world's gold and silver supply to act as a reserve base of national currencies.

Restoration of world trade is an important partner both in the means and in the result. Here also temporary exchange fixing is not the true answer. We must rather mitigate existing embargoes to make easier the exchange of products which one nation has and the other nation has not.

The Conference was called to better, and perhaps to cure, fundamental economic ills. It must not be diverted from that effort.

APPENDIX IV

THE EXCHANGE EQUALISATION FUND

Extracts from the evidence of Dr. O. W. Sprague, formerly Financial Adviser to the Bank of England, as given to the Sub-Committee of the House of Representatives on Banking and Currency, on February 22, 1934.

Mr. CROSS. Let me ask you a question there: Does not England do that [change the rates of prices at which to purchase gold], and has she not done it for years?

Dr. SPRAGUE. I should say not.

Mr. CROSS. Does she not have a fund with which she, at least, purchases dollars or other monetary units of other countries, when she finds a reason for stabilising values?

Dr. SPRAGUE. That is the so-called "equalisation account." I could tell you quite a bit about that, if you are interested in it.

Mr. CROSS. I am interested in it.

Dr. SPRAGUE. I can tell you of the principles that have been adopted in its management. England went off gold in September 1931 after making frantic efforts to remain on gold, and when it was clearly perceived that the situation was threatening.

Mr. CROSS. Let me state the point I have in mind: Did not England, when she went back on gold in 1925, have pound notes issued by the English Treasury, amounting at the end of the war to over £320,000,000, and is it not a fact that that issue was never fixed so as to be convertible into gold, but rather into securities or credits?

Dr. SPRAGUE. No.

Mr. CROSS. I have a limited knowledge of that, but that is what I gathered from the *Encyclopædia Britannica*.

Dr. SPRAGUE. The situation was this: During the war, one-pound and ten-shilling notes were issued. These were the lowest denomination. Five-pound currency notes were

253

issued before the war, and they were convertible into de-
nominations of one pound and ten shillings. Those notes were
notes of the Bank of England. When England returned to
the gold standard in 1925, the situation was the same as it
was before the war, with these two differences: At that time,
the one-pound and ten-shilling notes were in circulation instead of sovereigns and half-sovereigns, and you could not go
to the Bank of England and convert either bank balances or
notes into gold, except in large quantities. You could not get
gold coins, but you could get, with entire freedom, gold bars.

Mr. CROSS. On notes?

Mr. SPRAGUE. Yes; on notes.

Mr. CROSS. Then the statement in the *Encyclopædia
Britannica* is wrong.

Dr. SPRAGUE. Ordinarily those who wanted gold for
export would have bank balances that they would use instead
of notes, but if you accumulated enough notes to make it
worth while, you could get gold bars as well.

The theory was that the only real purpose, or the only
proper purpose, for gold was to meet foreign exchange
settlements, and to keep the currency under the gold pound
relatively to that of other countries, and we have the same
provision, practically, in our recent gold bill, which limits
the use of gold to international settlements. I think that
virtually all experts are in agreement, other than, perhaps,
some in France, that that is the only essential use for gold,
and that it is highly desirable in order to prevent individual
hoardings in periods of disturbance.

Mr. CROSS. Suppose you tell us about that fund, and
how they handle it?

Dr. SPRAGUE. It was clear that the pound was overvalued
in 1931, with an increase in British costs, which, relative
to the costs in other countries were high, with a resultant
shrinkage in the export trade of the country and an increasingly unfavourable balance of payments. Things did not
come to a head for some time because of the prestige of the
London market, which led people all over the world to
deposit money there. With a slight increase in the rates they
would bring in more money from the outside as long as

people continued to have confidence in the pound. In the spring of 1931 the situation was becoming difficult, because they were becoming to realise that a large volume of foreign assets held in the London market were more or less frozen. When the drain began—and it began in July—it was speedily found that there were no large volumes of foreign assets that could be liquidated to offset the drain of the with-drawals from London. First, the bank paid out gold that it had borrowed in New York and Paris, or privately borrowed in New York and Paris.

In fact, something like £200,000,000 had been used to meet the drain, and that at a moment when those special foreign borrowings of the Government and the bank were almost in exactly the same amount as the remaining gold in the Bank of England. There was no evidence of a cessation of the drain, and it was decided that it was inevitable that the country must go off gold. However, they made every effort to remain on gold, and they endeavoured to strengthen confidence by imposing additional taxation. They actually did balance their budget, and the budget has remained balanced ever since. Now, when the country went off gold, the pound at once dropped. It dropped somewhere between 20 and 25 per cent from its previous value. From that time to this, it has been the policy of the British Government to exert no influence calculated to depreciate the pound, but to endeavour to strengthen it and to smooth off the fluctua-tions. Then when it became evident, or when it became clear that the budget was balanced, the pound somewhat improved.

Mr. CROSS. I have heard several statements of it, but do you recall what the foreign or public debt of England amounts to?

Dr. SPRAGUE. About seven and a half billion pounds, which would be about $37,000,000,000, or at the old rate of exchange about thirty-seven and a half billion dollars. They have about one-third of the population of this country.

Mr. BUSBY. I have recently seen the statement that it amounted to thirty-seven and a half billion dollars. It would be approximately that under the old rate of exchange.

Dr. SPRAGUE. It is somewhere between seven and one-half

billion and eight billion pounds. It is perfectly prodigious in size, and the mass of the people there have to pay a heavy tax. If you have an income of $10,000 in England, you have to pay at least $2,000 in taxes.

Mr. CROSS. You say that the drain was so heavy in England that she had to go off the gold standard. As you know, the drain became terrific in all countries. Was that because of the inadequacy of the monetary base? That was true not only in England, but the drain became heavy here also.

Mr. BUSBY. It involved thirty-four countries in all.

Dr. SPRAGUE. They went off for different reasons and under different circumstances. I am simply saying that in the case of England, they made frantic efforts to stay on gold. They did not go off willingly.

Mr. CROSS. We were being drained heavily here.

Dr. SPRAGUE. But still we had a mass of gold which would have permitted us to go forward.

Mr. CROSS. Why?

Dr. SPRAGUE. It would have permitted us to go forward if we had wanted to do so.

Mr. CROSS. Why?

Dr. SPRAGUE. They went to the last sovereign that there was in the bank.

Mr. CROSS. Do you think that was wise?

Dr. SPRAGUE. I should say so in the case of the British Government, because they were the first country of any importance to go off gold. Their own self-respect demanded it, more than in the case of any other country that has gone off gold. Certain countries had imposed special restrictions on exchange, and, perhaps, any other country could go off gold without making the efforts which self-respect required in the case of the first country which took that step.

Mr. GOLDSBOROUGH. You used the term "self-respect": What do you have in mind there?

Dr. SPRAGUE. Well, if over a period of years you have had the reputation of meeting all of your engagements, and if people all over the world came to believe that you would, almost to a moral certainty, continue to do so, except in the case of war, you would feel, I think, that you must make every human effort to meet your engagements, and that, if you fail, it must be perfectly clear that it is physically impossible for you to do so.

Mr. GOLDSBOROUGH. What about the obligation of England to the great mass of her people, who, when she was on the gold, were out of work, and could not get work? How about her obligations to her own people?

Dr. SPRAGUE. If England could remain on the gold standard, and all other countries remain on gold, that would be well, but if disturbing influences were introduced over a period of extreme monetary uncertainty ——

Mr. GOLDSBOROUGH (interposing). With an internal debt as great as it was, and an external debt as great as it was existing all over the civilised world, how was it possible to have an economic recovery, except through bankruptcy, unless those various countries came off gold and raised their price levels?

Dr. SPRAGUE. If you take the English view, or the view that has been held—I would not say the English view, because there is no such thing, probably—but if you take the view that what is needed to bring about a price advance, or a high price level, is to increase confidence and to open up channels of trade, and to increase the demand for labour and materials, then you may be somewhat sceptical as to whether you should go very far by beginning the other way about it, with monetary measures. It has not greatly improved the British position to simply go off gold. It met the particular difficulty of further withdrawals of foreign money from the London market, but it did not greatly stimulate the trade of the country. That is partly because it was offset by additional quotas, and partly because it was offset by an adjustment of costs downward in the gold-standard countries, as, for example, in Belgium.

Dr. SPRAGUE. I believe you want to go back to the equalisation fund.

Mr. GOLDSBOROUGH. Personally, I would be very much interested to hear Dr. Sprague on the subject of the equalisation fund. I believe he made the statement that he had a lot to do with it.

Dr. SPRAGUE. I think I can explain it in a very short statement. After the country went off gold, and it became clear that the British Government was not disposed to do anything calculated to weaken the pound, but that it tended somewhat to improve the pound, at that time the purchase of dollars and francs began in order to pay off loans that had been secured. They were endeavouring to stay on gold, and in buying gold francs and gold dollars the policy was to buy gradually as the pound tended to appreciate, and to be ready to sell if the reverse movement came along. In the course of the winter and spring of 1932 a sufficient amount of dollars and francs were acquired to pay the loans that had been secured, or the loans of £130,000,000 that had been secured in Paris and New York. Then the question presented itself as to what to do, after that stage had been reached. There was no authority on the part of the bank or the treasury to buy additional foreign currency for any particular purpose, and the bank certainly was not disposed to do that and incur the risk involved.

Consequently, it was decided to grant authority to deal in foreign exchange up to £150,000,000, which meant that the same thing could be done that was done while these loans were unpaid; and the same policy was adopted of taking no position about what the true value of the pound was, but when the pound tended to appreciate, to buy. It was the policy not to hold it, but to buy gradually, and then, if the pound tended to decline, to begin to sell those dollars and francs so as to keep it from declining below the level which, it was believed, would not continue. Now, there was one occasion, in November 1932, when, after having been selling francs and dollars because the pound was weak, the stock of francs and dollars was almost exhausted. This fund does not do you any good in keeping currency from depreciating unless you have francs and dollars already on hand.

Mr. GOLDSBOROUGH. What is the art by which you sell francs and dollars?

Dr. SPRAGUE. This was entirely handled, so far as the technical part of it was concerned, through the Bank of

England. The bank would buy foreign exchange, or drafts on Paris and drafts on New York, and those drafts would be credited to the account of the Bank of England in the various banks of France and the Federal Reserve Bank of New York, or other agencies, just as any commercial banks might do. The policy that the bank was instructed to follow was to use its best judgment to keep the pound as steady as possible, and that if there were strong influences favouring either an upward or downward movement of the pound sterling, the bank should take cognisance of that, and try to adjust the situation as well as it could. As I have said, in November 1932 the stock of francs and dollars was so nearly exhausted that they were fast ceasing to exist, and the exchange took its own course. It dropped to $3.15, not because the Government had desired it to drop to that point, but because the forces against it were very strong. The reverse of that situation obtained at the beginning of last year.

First, in the case of the franc, and then in the case of the dollar, both currencies were weak against sterling at the rates which then obtained, which were about $3.25 to the pound, and sterling was allowed to rise. The dollar and franc were being purchased, until the pound reached the point of $3.45. The exodus from the country was becoming very strong in February of last year. Then the question that was up to those who were managing the fund was this: Shall we take our hand off and buy no more dollars, and let sterling go where it will, or shall we buy dollars to, at least, moderate the upward tendency. The latter policy was adopted, because it was believed that the outflow from the banks was temporary. It was felt that as soon as the reverse movement set in, if we did nothing, the pound would shoot up, and then would reverse and would come down, which was contrary to the policy of the Government. That involved last February a very heavy purchase of dollars, a part of which was earmarked for gold in the Federal Reserve Bank in New York. However, it was not felt that this was damaging to the United States, because it was believed that with the outflow, if it did not go into sterling, it would go into other currencies.

It was believed that if sterling had gone up to a level where it was generally believed would not hold, the outflow from this country would have gone into French francs, Swiss francs, or Dutch guilders.

That is all there is in the conduct of this account.

Mr. CROSS. Why was it increased? At first it was £150,000,000.

Dr. SPRAGUE. It was like this: the movement of funds between countries seemed to become increasingly large, and we simply thought that it was a safeguard. You cannot tell how much foreign currency you may need to buy in order to maintain a reasonable stability for sterling; so it was felt that we ought to sell enough to have a sufficient margin so we could operate. Among other reasons, there is a very large speculative movement possible against or in favour of any particular currency. One cannot exactly measure that, but it runs into a large number of millions of pounds, perhaps £50,000,000 or more. That would be a purely speculative operation against any currency which, for any reason whatever, appears to be strongly or weakly quoted, or that tends to move either upward or downward.

As you see, the objective of the British policy in this matter was comparatively narrow. If they had attempted to fix the price of sterling at some figure relative to the dollar and the franc, which would have been impossible, they would have required an immense fund. However, that has not been the objective in view at any time.

Our stabilisation fund is different from the British in two respects. In the first place, the British equalisation fund is not a fund, but it is simply an account. The proper phrase would be an equalisation account. It is simply an authority to employ £150,000,000 or £350,000,000 for this purpose.

Mr. CROSS. It is now £350,000,000.

Dr. SPRAGUE. Yes. It is an authority to employ it for the purpose of steadying the exchanges. It does not exist as ready money. If purchases of foreign currencies are made, that means that at that time the British Government must borrow some money in order to provide the means of payment. It is just the same way as with our various appropriations, where you authorise expenditures for various purposes, or for all the various departments and agencies of the Government.

The British equalisation account is simply an authorisation to employ for this particular purpose a certain amount of money. Now, our fund is an actual honest-to-goodness quantity of money. It does physically exist, so that when and if it is employed, it does not involve raising money in the money market, as is the case with any such use of the British equalisation account. In the second place, our fund, I take it, has no such occasion for use as the British account. In fact, I am not at all certain that it will be used at all in the foreign exchange market, owing to the fact that we have gone back on gold at the new parity. Consequently, if the dollar moves in either direction away from the gold point, gold will be imported or exported. That does not require the use of the fund at all.[1]

Mr. CROSS. We are not really on the gold standard now, are we?

Dr. SPRAGUE. We are on a modified gold standard.

Mr. CROSS. Do you mean that, in fact, there is good paper redemption in gold?

Dr. SPRAGUE. As I understand the new bill, if the dollar were to rise to the export point, gold exports would be permitted.

Mr. CROSS. I cannot see much difference between them, because England has the power to expend for the purchase of foreign exchange £350,000,000. The difference is between having it piled up, as we have it, or raising it. We have ours on hand, but England will get hers if she needs it.

Dr. SPRAGUE. Yes. There is this very great difference, as I see it, that we have the actual money, and we can use it for certain other purposes, such, for example, as the purchase of Government securities. Obviously, the British fund cannot do that, because in order to get the money to buy Government securities, the Government, in the first place, would have to issue some Government securities to provide

---

[1] See Supplementary Note on p. 242.

the money. Our fund has a use, although it is called a stabilisation fund, far beyond the possible use, or the conditions of use, of the English equalisation account. As I see, it has a particular function in the matter of foreign exchange. They are not only permitted to accept gold at $35 per ounce, but the law also provides for the granting of licences to export gold in the event the dollar moves to the export point. I believe that is surplusage as a part of the gold bill. It is really only important in connection with Government finances, and its use for internal purposes.

Mr. CROSS. If this country should manage, with the amount of gold we have, and we are really getting more of it, to get a large volume of the silver in the world in our Treasury, would not that necessarily force the other countries to meet us around the table and agree to fix a ratio between the two metals? They would be in a position where they would not be able to get either metal in large quantities.

Dr. SPRAGUE. I do not believe you could force upon them a monetary system.

Mr. CROSS. If we had all the gold, and they could not stay on the gold standard, they would have to adopt the silver standard or some other standard.

Dr. SPRAGUE. They might, if I may use the expression, thumb their noses at us. You cannot expect to force the rest of the world to adopt a monetary arrangement which is not in the interest of the rest of the world. If you will act in running the monetary system practically as you would act if you were on the gold, you can get virtually all of the advantages of being on gold. Therefore, in my judgment, if Great Britain to-day, in the management of its Government finances, its credit policies, and its capital investment policies, did practically what it would do if on gold, they would get practically the same results. The danger is that countries will not do that.

Mr. CROSS. If they had no gold, and there was no probability of their ever going back on the gold standard, and if they knew there was no chance of doing that, and that they would always have unconvertible paper, do you not think that would have a terrific effect upon them?

Dr. SPRAGUE. It would have an effect which could, I think, be overcome gradually, and, perhaps, speedily, if the world were convinced that the British Government would go forward on virtually the same line that it has followed during the last two years. One does not know how the pound will be revalued when the world goes back to gold, but there is very great confidence in the pound sterling.

That confidence, I should say, arises in the main, or is the result in the main, of the policy which has been pursued by the British Government since that country went off gold. Whether it has been a wise policy from the industrial point of view or not, it has strengthened the financial confidence, or the confidence of financial circles around the world in the pound sterling.

Mr. CROSS. They are better manipulators than we are. They are better financiers than we are.

Dr. SPRAGUE. Yes; they have taken what they call a neutral policy with regard to the value of the pound. It has operated so that influential financial circles have felt that the pound certainly can be made reasonably stable. Through a certain process of trial and error, an equilibrium may be reached, so that the value of the pound would be determined. The great difficulty has resulted from the countries that went back to gold in 1925, and which went back at rates which were not equilibrium rates. The pound was overvalued, and it is being restored to its old parity.

The British costs were resistant, causing a necessary reduction to bring the costs into equilibrium. The French undervalued the franc somewhat, and Italy overvalued the lira. They had a struggle between the countries in an endeavour to regain or re-establish equilibrium for their currencies, which was manifested in a variety of schemes, such as quotas, additional tariff restrictions, and so forth. It will not be possible to sit around the table and determine and get an agreement upon proper equilibrium rates for the various currencies. I believe that can only be determined by a process of trial and error, during a period in which a more or less neutral policy is adopted by the different countries, so that their various currencies can reach levels appropriate to the world situation. If prices go up rapidly in this country relatively to prices in other countries, then we shall get a firm foundation under our revaluation of the dollar. If they do not go up, we shall continue to weaken the currencies of other countries, because of our revaluation at the point at which it is revalued, to an extent far greater than the undermining influence exerted in the case of the French franc in 1927.

INDEX